102nd U.S. Open Championship

Bethpage State Park

June 13-16, 2002

102nd
U.S. OPEN
Bethpage State Park

Writer: Robert Sommers   Photographers: Michael Cohen, Phil Inglis   Editor: Bev Norwood

ISBN 1-878843-36-2

©2002 United States Golf Association®
Golf House, Far Hills, N.J. 07931

Statistics produced by Unisys Corporation

Photograph on page 7 by AP/Wide World Photos
Course photography by Fred Vuich
Course illustrations by Dan Wardlaw © The Majors of Golf

Published by IMG Worldwide Inc.,
1360 East Ninth Street, Cleveland, Ohio 44114

Designed and produced by Davis Design

Printed in the United States of America

102nd

U.S. OPEN

Official Annual Presented by

ROLEX

Maybe it wasn't exactly a foregone conclusion, but it would be hard to find anybody in the know in golf who was surprised when Tiger Woods won his second United States Open Championship in June of 2002. Woods, who was exposed to a variety of public courses in his formative years, certainly seemed at home in New York's Bethpage State Park on Long Island, although, thanks to a multi-million-dollar upgrade financed by the USGA, the course was a far cry from your average municipal course. The USGA's decision several years earlier to break new ground by staging America's 102nd national championship on a municipal course for the first time in its 108-year history certainly seemed to bear fruit.

The years of preparation at Bethpage presented the world's greatest players with a true test and the cream came to the top. Tiger won decisively — the only man to break par with his 277 and for just the sixth time in Open history, including his victory at Pebble Beach in 2000, he was the sole leader after each round. But two of his most persistent challengers — Phil Mickelson and Sergio Garcia — and two starting bogeys the last day brought out the competitive best in the game's most dominant player of today in the intense final round.

All of this and much more — the conditioning and set-up of the course, the raucous crowds, the heavy weather — are detailed in this 18th annual commemorative book presented by Rolex and the USGA, along with a marvelous gallery of exclusive photographs. These books are true treasures.

Arnold Palmer

102nd
U.S. OPEN
9/11 Tribute

Scrabbling through the rubble of the World Trade Center seven months after the terrorists struck, John Caputo, a retired New York City firefighter, spotted something white. At first he thought it could be a bone from one of the nearly 3,000 victims massacred in the attack. Digging deeper, Caputo pulled out not a bone but a nice, white golf ball.

He was stunned. Speaking at a press conference the day before the 2002 U.S. Open Championship began, Caputo said, "I just couldn't believe that out of all this destruction, something like a golf ball could survive."

That golf ball has been enshrined in the USGA's museum in Far Hills, N.J., handed over to Reed Mackenzie, the association's president, by nine-year-old Joseph Vigiano, one of two sons of police detective Joseph Vigiano, killed when the twin towers collapsed.

The golf ball and fire department flags.

This was a poignant moment for the Vigianos, not only for young Joseph and his eight-year-old brother, Jimmy, but for their grandfather as well. Fire Department captain John Vigiano lost two sons — Joseph and his brother John, a city firefighter.

Besides Caputo and the Vigianos, Governor George Pataki attended the ceremony wearing a golf shirt and a baseball cap carrying the slogan "I ♥ New York," along with Bernadette Castro, the New York State Parks Commissioner, Nicholas Scoppetta, New York City Fire Commissioner, and a number of uniformed fire department officials.

They had come to Bethpage to accept a gift from the USGA.

When the terrorists struck and set the twin towers ablaze, fire trucks raced to the World Trade Center. Then the towers collapsed, killing the Vigiano brothers and many others and destroying fire trucks and emergency medical service ambulances.

So vital are those ambulances, they answer more than a million calls a year; lose one, lose lives.

Speaking for the USGA, Mackenzie announced the USGA would replace an ambulance.

Explaining the reasoning behind the gift, Mackenzie said, "In the months following the attack, the volunteers and staff of the USGA searched for an appropriate symbol to honor the heroism of so many New York firefighters and the people whose lives were so directly affected by them.

"Searching for an appropriate response, we looked to USGA history and found two instances when the association helped buy ambulances, both of them in times of terror. During the Second World War the USGA gave one to the town of St. Andrews, Scotland, and the other to Pearl Harbor. With those in mind, the USGA today makes a similar contribu-

USGA President Reed Mackenzie accepted the golf ball from Joseph Vigiano and his younger brother Jimmy.

tion to the Fire Department of New York.

"In presenting this ambulance, all of us salute the city where the USGA was founded in 1894, and we thank the community of New York for being our host for this year's United States Open Championship.

"When we remember that many New York firefighters and emergency medical teams regularly play at Bethpage, and that many of them are USGA members, we feel this venue and this championship provide the most suitable and appropriate place for such a gesture."

The USGA's ambulance will carry a plaque inscribed:

From The United States Golf Association
To the City and People of New York
In Remembrance of 9/11/01

The first hole, par 4 and 430 yards.

W hen Robert Moses lost the 1934 New York gubernatorial election to Herbert Lehman by an overwhelming margin, the voters had done him a favor. Instead of a risky career in elective politics, Moses kept on as he had for the past decade — expanding and consolidating a secure power base through non-elective appointments.

Since 1924, governors and mayors had appointed Moses to such offices as New York City Parks Commissioner, chairman of the Long Island state parks commission, chairman of the New York State Power Authority, sole member of the New York City Parkway authority and the biggest prize of them all, chairman of the Consolidated Triborough Bridge and City Tunnel Authority.

Through 44 years, Moses used these offices — at one time he held 12 simultaneously — to build broader authority than he would have commanded as governor. Robert A. Caro, his biographer, claims Moses held more power than the governor of the state and mayor of the city combined.

A master manipulator, he sat on some commissions that proposed projects and others that approved them. He couldn't lose. In office for what seemed a lifetime, Moses re-shaped New York.

He hovered over the state and the city from 1924 until 1968, holding on by using a simple tactic; when he ran into opposition, he threatened to resign. Politicians usually backed down. Gradually,

Robert Moses

though, his strategy wore thin, his influence eroded and offices slipped away.

Finally Governor Nelson Rockefeller had had enough and relieved him of the Triborough Bridge Authority, his last position. Moses had reached the age of 79 by then. Such was his power to intimidate, he had clung to office 14 years beyond mandatory retirement age. He died in July of 1987, at 92.

Tall and athletic — he swam for Yale as an undergraduate — Moses developed an agile and creative mind. He earned degrees not only from Yale but from Oxford and Columbia as well.

Furthermore, he was different. A son of privilege, he pledged as a young man to devote his life to public service. He did indeed, and he served nearly *pro bono* late in his career, accepting only an annual salary of $25,000 as New York parks commissioner.

Not that he didn't live well. What with fully-staffed offices all over town, a fleet of chauffeur-driven limousines and a cornucopian expense account, he didn't need much else.

Still, he was a man on a mission. Moses used his authority to build roads, like the West Side Highway; bridges, such as the Triborough and the Verrazano Narrows, and the Brooklyn-Battery tunnel. He built Jones Beach State Park, and he saved The Little Red Lighthouse Under The Great Gray Bridge. He put together the 1964 World's Fair, cleared slums and built housing projects. He built an airline terminal in Manhattan, added improvements to Central Park and in the process saved an old-time carousel and rebuilt the Central Park Zoo.

A man of wide-ranging interests, Moses built Shea Stadium, the New York Coliseum and the Lincoln Center for the Performing Arts, and without him the United Nations might not have settled in New York.

While he never learned to drive, he built the Brooklyn-Queens, the Grand Central, the Cross Bronx, the Cross Island, the Hutchinson River, the Major Deegan, the Staten Island, the Throgs Neck, the Whitestone and the Van Wyck Expressways. And

1st
PAR 4
430 YARDS

2nd
PAR 4
389 YARDS

he built the Robert Moses Expressway.

He built parks — lots of parks. Extending his reach to Long Island, Moses built Montauk State Park, at the eastern tip of the island, and Owl's Head, at the far western end. In between he built Valley Stream, Hempstead Lake, Belmont Lake, Gilgo, Wildwood, Orient Beach, Hither Hills, Massapequa, Sunken Meadows and Robert Moses State Park.

And 35 miles from midtown Manhattan, smack alongside the Bethpage State Parkway, which he built, connected on the south by the Southern State Parkway, which he built, and on the north by the Northern State Parkway, which he built, and close to the Long Island Expressway, a work of his the comedian Alan King often called the world's longest parking lot, Robert Moses built Bethpage State

Park, a recreational Xanadu for the non-country club set.

Moses did nothing on a small scale. In building Bethpage he turned 1,368 acres of rolling woodland and farmland into a working man's happy valley of tennis courts, polo fields, picnic grounds and miles of bridle paths centered around a lavish clubhouse longer than a football field, with men's and women's locker rooms, men's and women's lounges and card rooms, private dining rooms, a main dining room and a grill room.

The property came with one golf course, Lenox Hills, a private club that had failed. Moses added three more — the Red, the Blue and the jewel of them all, the Black.

In June of 2002, the USGA took the United

3rd
PAR 3
205 YARDS

The second hole, par 4 and 389 yards.

States Open to Bethpage Black, the first Open ever played over a municipal course. The championship had been played over courses open to the public in the past, but both Pebble Beach, which has seen three, and Pinehurst charge more than $300 a round. A swing around Bethpage Black costs less than $40.

Idealistic, persuasive and inexhaustible, Moses let nothing stand in his way — not the political clout of governors or mayors, not the blistering prose of crusading reporters, not even, in the case of Bethpage, the indisputable fact that New York didn't have the money. Moses built this Land of Cockaigne in the bleakest days of the Great Depression of the 1930s, when money was as scarce as Saharan monsoons.

He did it because, along with his other management and promotional legerdemain, Moses had the luxury of luck. Just then a gaggle of federal agencies had begun throwing money around to put thousands of the unemployed to work building roads, bridges, public buildings, airports and recreational facilities. They built Hoover Dam, for example, and they also built playgrounds, swimming pools, tennis courts and lots of golf courses and clubhouses. They did them right. They built such an elegant clubhouse at the George Wright municipal course, in Bos-

4th
PAR 5
517 YARDS

9

The fifth hole, par 4 and 451 yards.

5th
PAR 4
451 YARDS

into actually using their picks and shovels. But when it was finished, Mount Pleasant, a municipal course, turned out one of the three or four best courses between Merion, in Philadelphia, and Pinehurst, in North Carolina.

Hook designed Mount Pleasant himself, but these were difficult times for everyone, certainly for the golf course architect, a largely unappreciated breed at the time. Hardly anyone had heard of Donald Ross, Perry Maxwell, Alister MacKenzie, Billy Bell, Chandler Egan, William Bruce Langford, Robert Trent Jones, or A.W. Tillinghast, names that grace many of our greatest golfing grounds. Yet during the Depression they too worked on some of these government-financed projects.

Relief agencies built hundreds. Bethpage Black was among the best. It should have been; it has an impeccable pedigree. It bears the imprimatur of Tillinghast, an outlandish character yet gifted golf course architect.

The spoiled son of a well-off Philadelphia family that made its money in the rubber business, Tillinghast bragged that he never finished a school he attended — he either quit or was tossed out — and he ran with a crowd his grandson described as a "cadre of rogues —

ton, both the mayor of Boston and the governor of Massachusetts commandeered space for offices.

The George Wright clubhouse was built by the Works Progress Administration (WPA). Bethpage began as a product of the Civil Works Administration (CWA), a make-work brainchild of Harry Hopkins, a former social worker who sat at the right hand of President Franklin Roosevelt. Eventually, the CWA evolved into the WPA, and Hopkins headed it as well.

These work-relief programs emphasized hand labor. Golf course construction had to be pick-and-shovel work — no heavy machinery unless muscle couldn't do the job. It was tough work for the crews and tough for the foremen. Perhaps because these were such grim times, the men figured the quicker they finished, the sooner they would be out of work. Even though their wages weren't much — they averaged a little more than $50 a month — any job was better than none. People of that era found welfare embarrassing.

Workers dawdled nonetheless. Charles A. (Gus) Hook recalled building Mount Pleasant golf course, in Baltimore. As foreman he had to bully his men

6th
PAR 4
408 YARDS

7th
PAR 4
489 YARDS

The eighth hole, par 3 and 210 yards.

wealthy, arrogant, flashy, reckless, heavy-drinking playboys."

Nevertheless, he was extremely well-read and an accomplished conversationalist. He knew everyone. The walls of his mansion were lined with photographs signed, for example, "To Albert," or "To Bertie with love" from the likes of Lillian Russell, Thomas Edison and Jack Dempsey. Visiting Mexico City with his wife, Lillian, Tillinghast was hailed by a rumpled looking man who called him by name. They chatted for a while, then Tillie invited him to lunch. The man spoke in broken English, and when he left without an introduction, Lillian asked who he might be. According to Dr. Philip Brown,

the grandson, Tillinghast answered, "Some Russian refugee — Leon Trotsky." Tillinghast had other talents as well. During the 1930s, after the golf-course building boom of the 1920s had dried up, he wrote for and edited the magazine *Golf Illustrated*, a glossy, large-format magazine of the 1920s and 1930s, contributed to almost every known golf magazine of the time, did some photography, wrote fiction and dabbled in antiques. His legacy, though, rests not in his literature but in the golf courses he conceived.

Tillie had taken to golf in the late 1890s and

8*th*
PAR 3
210 YARDS

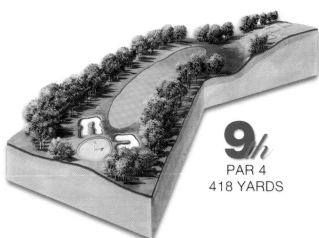

9th
PAR 4
418 YARDS

10th
PAR 4
492 YARDS

11th
PAR 4
435 YARDS

in Toledo, a Donald Ross design.

How much time he put into Bethpage remains uncertain. As consulting architect, Tillinghast leaves hints he drew up the plans and laid out the routing, but recent revisionists suggest Tillinghast had little to do with Bethpage and that the credit should go to Joe Burbeck, the state engineer. Who knows?

It's likely that Tillinghast did what most architects of the period did. He drew up the design, then left, leaving the construction work to Burbeck. This was common practice. Could Donald Ross have done 500 courses if he had hung around to oversee construction?

It is possible as well, that, as his son claims, Burbeck did the actual designing and that, as consulting architect, Tillinghast simply looked over Burbeck's shoulder and clucked approval.

Without question, though, Tillinghast left the construction work to Burbeck, who, Tillinghast stated, "was in daily direction of the entire work from the start to its finish."

Tillinghast credits Burbeck as well for suggesting one of the Bethpage courses should be a man-killer. Tillie agreed and turned the Black into a fierce test of golf. So tough was it at its birth, Tillinghast himself had reservations about some holes, especially the fourth, an uphill par 5 commanded by a huge cross-bunker threatening the drive and a smaller version blocking the entrance to a shallow green that falls away from the shot.

grew into a rather good player, which gave him a leg up in understanding what a golf course should be. He used his feel for the game and an acute aesthetic sense to give us some of our most playable and scenically pleasing courses — both the East and West Courses at Winged Foot, in Mamaroneck, N.Y.; Ridgewood and the Upper and Lower courses at Baltusrol, in northern New Jersey; San Francisco Golf Club; the East Course at the Baltimore Country Club's Five Farms complex; Brook Hollow, in Dallas; Seaview, near Atlantic City, N.J.; Quaker Ridge, in Westchester County, N.Y., and Brackenridge Park, a public course in San Antonio where the PGA Tour played the Texas Open for many years.

These are his best-known works, but he did lots more and remodeled others, like Inverness Club,

The 12th hole, par 4 and 499 yards.

The 13th hole, par 5 and 554 yards.

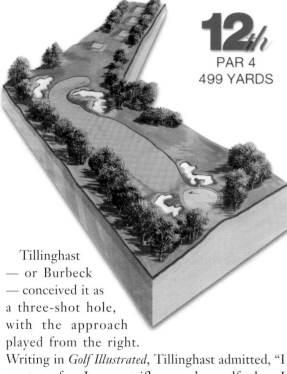

12th
PAR 4
499 YARDS

Tillinghast
— or Burbeck
— conceived it as
a three-shot hole,
with the approach
played from the right.
Writing in *Golf Illustrated*, Tillinghast admitted, "I must confess I was a trifle scared myself when I looked back and regarded the hazardous route that must be taken by a stinging second shot to get into position to attack this green."

Although it measured just 517 yards, it played much more difficult for the Open field than Tillinghast could have imagined. Scores averaged above par; no one could remember a par-5 hole so tough to beat.

The Bethpage Black that Tillinghast and Burbeck built and the public played for more than 60 years was not the same as the course the Open field played. Like so many of our great courses, the Black had to be

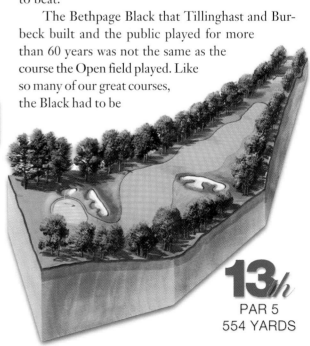

13th
PAR 5
554 YARDS

To polish this one-time gem to Open standards, the USGA pumped $3.5 million into revising the Black. It was the first time the association had spent its own money on course preparations. Costs had always been left to the club, but Bethpage had no club in the usual sense. The USGA's money went largely into reconstruction. The State kicked in more for conditioning and maintenance.

When he looked over the Black, Jones realized he needed sand for the bunkers. In a spectacular six-month *magnum opus* of logistics, truckers shuttled

14th
PAR 3
161 YARDS

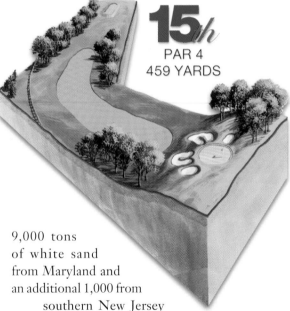

15th
PAR 4
459 YARDS

lengthened and reworked for the Open. Again, as so many over the last decade or so, the reworking was done by Rees Jones. It wasn't easy.

When the idea blossomed in the early 1990s, the Black's condition could most kindly be described as needy. Some dedicated and enthusiastic patrons have called it ratty. During the middle of the 1980s, the Long Island State Park Commission asked Frank Duane, another golf course architect, to evaluate the Bethpage golf courses. His assessment and recommendations ran 35 pages.

The Black's condition was no secret to the USGA, which, spurred by David Fay, the organization's executive director, had been pushing to move the national championship to a municipal course for some years.

9,000 tons of white sand from Maryland and an additional 1,000 from southern New Jersey right through New York City and out to Long Island. It was quite a stunt. To avoid the worst of the city's chaotic traffic, truckers timed their trips to cross New York's bridges at dawn and dusk, with traffic at its thinnest. It was worth the effort; those gleaming white bunkers define the reborn Black Course. Looking it over when the job had been done, Jones declared, "Bethpage Black is about sand."

Comparing aerial photographs of Bethpage's early days with its condition in the 1990s showed that over the years, trees had grown in some bunkers and that others had disappeared, filled in, or shrunk away from greens they had been built to protect.

16th
PAR 4
479 YARDS

The 14th hole, par 3 and 161 yards.

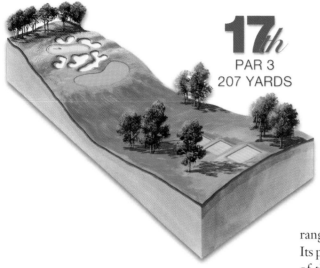

17th
PAR 3
207 YARDS

kers into one huge Tillinghast-style purgatory.

When he finished he had added punch to a design that had become outdated by modern clubs that propel today's balls ever farther.

Still, Rees had plenty to work with, for in the Black he had a design of wide variety. Some holes play uphill, some play downhill, some swing right, some swing left and some run dead straight.

It has short par 4s and long par 4s, a pair of reachable par 5s and four severely bunkered par 3s with dangerous hole locations that in themselves could settle the championship. They range from the 161-yard 14th to the 210-yard eighth. Its par 5s measure from 517 to 554 yards, within reach of the modern golfer's second shots, and its par 4s measure from 389 yards to 499 yards, the longest admitted length of a par-4 hole in Open history.

In what might be remembered as his finest reconstruction, Rees created an essentially new 18th hole by moving the tee back and salting the route with bunkers that both tease and dare the golfer to make a choice of what kind of shot and what route to take. This inspired move turned what had been an entirely forgettable home hole — nothing more than a means of leading the golfer from the 17th green to the clubhouse — into a tempting and testing close to the 2002 championship.

In the restoration process, the cross-bunker of the fourth grew to startling dimensions and Jones added another huge expanse that blocks the direct line to the green.

Other swatches wriggle snakelike alongside fairways; those separating the 10th and 11th fairways seem to serpentine all the way from tee to green.

Tim Moraghan, the USGA's championship agronomist, estimates he spread 12 to 13 acres of sand in rebuilding, replacing and expanding Bethpage's 71 bunkers. They are indeed large and deep.

By the time the first blow was struck, the sand had been in place three years, for this was no overnight metamorphosis. Jones, Fay and everyone deeply involved had spent six years turning a typically overplayed and under-maintained municipal course into a picturesque and stern challenge to golf's virtuosi.

In bringing the fairways and greens up to standard, the Bethpage grounds crew first killed off weeds and crabgrass, then sowed perennial ryegrass seed at a rate of 600 to 800 pounds per acre. Considering one application every year for six years, crews spread roughly 3,500 to 4,000 pounds over each acre of mown grass.

As the grass grew, Jones tinkered with every hole. He shrank some greens, expanded others to set up new hole locations, then blocked the easy approach by sweeping bunkers close to swallow the mis-played shot. On one hole Jones conjoined three small bun-

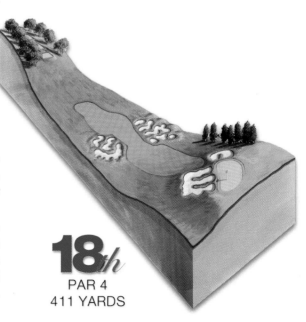

18th
PAR 4
411 YARDS

The 17th hole, par 3 and 207 yards.

Greg Norman, whose first U.S. Open was 1979, qualified for his 19th championship. He had placed second twice.

102nd
U.S. OPEN
Qualifying

On the morning of June 4, Greg Norman helicoptered across Florida from his home on Jupiter Island to Tampa for two rounds of golf because he wanted to play in the 2002 U.S. Open. No longer one of the game's premier players, Norman had to qualify.

One day earlier, at the Columbine Country Club, near Denver, Derek Tolan qualified as well.

Norman is a 47-year-old seasoned professional, once the finest player in the game. Tolan was a 16-year-old amateur, the youngest player in the field. Besides placing second in two Opens, Norman had won two British Opens. In his finest moment, Tolan won the Arizona Junior Classic. How good you've been doesn't matter; it's what you can do now that counts.

One of four qualifiers at Tampa, Norman led a field of 77. Tolan won one of two places in a field of 31 in Denver.

Nor was Norman alone among prominent players forced to qualify. Wayne Grady and Bob Tway, both former PGA champions, made it as well.

Qualifying has become a rite of passage for ambitious golfers driven to compete at the game's highest levels. It debuted when 165 players entered the 1913 championship, far too many to play two rounds on one day. To pare the field to 64, half played 36 holes for 32 places one day, half the next. Fortunately for history, Francis Ouimet, Harry Vardon and Ted Ray made it.

By 2002, though, entries had grown to 8,468 zealots. Instead of having that horde all play Bethpage Black, all but 208 men played 18 holes at one of the 105 sites scattered about the country. Of those, 564 advanced to 12 sectional qualifying sites, where they joined 208 others exempt from the first stage and played 36 holes for 81 spots.

An additional 75 players avoided both qualifying stages through outstanding recent playing records or through invitations based on distinguished careers.

Felix Casas of the Philippines then got in as an alternate after the withdrawal of Bruce Fleisher, who had qualifed as the 2001 U.S. Senior Open champion.

With the odds against winning stacked heavily against any but a fully exempt player, it has happened. Ken Venturi went through both stages and won the 1964 Open, and five years later Orville Moody pulled it off as well.

Since then only Steve Jones, the 1996 champion, had survived even one qualifying round.

Nevertheless, they try, and while they rarely win, some develop into champions. Back in 1931, 19-year-old Byron Nelson and 18-year-old Ben Hogan began their Open careers in the Dallas qualifier. Theirs were not successful debuts. A score of 151 qualified; Hogan shot 165 and Nelson withdrew after an opening 80. They persisted and grew into two of the greatest golfers of them all.

Arnold Palmer qualified in 1953 and 1954, and Jack Nicklaus in 1957 and 1958. Both had exemptions after that, although Palmer had to go through sectional qualifying in 1955 and Nicklaus in 1959.

Nicklaus never had to qualify again, but Palmer kept at it after his exemptions ran out. He qualified in 1977, 1979, 1981 and 1982, but tried and failed every year from 1984 through 1989.

Palmer didn't try again, but others will, and perhaps blossom into champions as well.

Players Who Were Fully Exempt for the 2002 U.S. Open (75)

Michael Allen	8	Retief Goosen	1, 8, 10, 11,	Paul McGinley	10, 17
Robert Allenby	9, 17		14, 17	Rocco Mediate	8, 17
Billy Andrade	17	Padraig Harrington	10, 17	Phil Mickelson	8, 9, 11, 17
Paul Azinger	8, 17	Dudley Hart	17	Colin Montgomerie	10, 17
Thomas Bjorn	10, 17	Scott Hoch	9, 12, 17	Jose Maria Olazabal	3, 11, 17
Mark Brooks	8	David Howell	10	Peter O'Malley	16
Angel Cabrera	8, 10, 17	Hale Irwin	13	Mark O'Meara	3, 4
Mark Calcavecchia	9, 17	Toshi Izawa	15, 17	Jesper Parnevik	17
Michael Campbell	10, 17	Lee Janzen	1	Craig Parry	16
Stewart Cink	8, 9, 17	Steve Jones	1	Corey Pavin	1
Darren Clarke	10, 17	Robert Karlsson	10	Craig Perks	6
Jose Coceres	17	Shingo Katayama	15, 17	Kenny Perry	9, 17
John Cook	17	Jerry Kelly	17	Nick Price	11, 17
John Daly	17	Tom Kite	1, 8	Adam Scott	10, 17
Chris DiMarco	9, 11, 17	Matt Kuchar	17	Vijay Singh	3, 5, 8, 9, 11, 17
Joe Durant	9	Bernhard Langer	9, 10, 17	Jeff Sluman	9
David Duval	4, 9, 17	Paul Lawrie	4, 10	Steve Stricker	9
Ernie Els	1, 9, 10, 11, 14, 17	Tom Lehman	9, 17	Kevin Sutherland	17
Bob Estes	9, 12, 17	Justin Leonard	4, 9, 17	Hal Sutton	9
Nick Faldo	13	Frank Lickliter	9	David Toms	5, 9, 11, 12, 17
Niclas Fasth	10, 17	Davis Love III	5, 8, 9, 17	Kirk Triplett	8
Brad Faxon	9, 17	Steve Lowery	9	Scott Verplank	9, 17
Bruce Fleisher[(W)]	7	Shigeki Maruyama	11, 12, 17	Mike Weir	9, 17
Jim Furyk	9, 17	Len Mattiace	17	Tiger Woods	1, 3, 4, 5, 8, 9,
Sergio Garcia	8, 9, 12, 17	Billy Mayfair	9		11, 12, 17
Matt Gogel	8	Scott McCarron	9, 17		

Key to Player Exemptions:

1 Winners of the U.S. Open Championship for the last 10 years
2 Winner of the 2001 U.S. Amateur Championship
3 Winners of the Masters Tournament the last five years
4 Winners of the British Open Championship the last five years
5 Winners of the PGA of America Championship the last five years
6 Winner of the 2002 Players Championship
7 Winner of the 2001 U.S. Senior Open Championship
8 From the 2001 U.S. Open Championship, the 15 lowest scorers and anyone tying for 15th place
9 From the 2001 final official PGA Tour money list, the top 30 money leaders
10 From the 2001 final official PGA European Tour, the top 15 money leaders
11 From the 2002 official PGA Tour money list, the top 10 money leaders through May 26
12 Any multiple winner of PGA Tour co-sponsored events whose victories are considered official from April 25, 2001 through June 2, 2002
13 Special exemptions selected by the USGA Executive Committee; International players not otherwise exempt as selected by the USGA Executive Committee
14 From the 2002 PGA European Tour, the top two money leaders through May 27
15 From the 2001 final Japan Golf Tour money list, the top two leaders provided they are within the top 75 point leaders of the World Rankings at that time
16 From the 2001-2002 official PGA Tour of Australasia money list as of March 18, the top two leaders provided they are within the top 75 point leaders of the World Rankings at that time
17 From the final World Rankings list, the top 50 point leaders as of May 27

[(W)] Withdrew

Sectional Qualifying Results

Lake Merced Golf and Country Club
Daly City, Calif.
70 players for 3 qualifying spots
Andy Miller, Napa, Calif., 67-68–135
*Ricky Barnes, Stockton, Calif., 70-67–137
Paul Goydos, Trabuco Canyon, Calif., 66-72–138
Felix Casas, Philippines, 68-72–140 (alternate)

Columbine Country Club
Denver, Colo.
31 players for 2 qualifying spots
*Ben Portie, Westminster, Colo., 68-67–135
(P)*Derek Tolan, Highlands Ranch, Colo., 70-69–139

Woodmont Country Club
Rockville, Md.
203 players for 34 qualifying spots
Peter Lonard, Australia, 65-63–128
Blaine McCallister, Ponte Vedra Beach, Fla., 67-64-131
Pete Jordan, Valrico, Fla., 65-67–132
Joey Sindelar, Horseheads, N.Y., 64-68–132
Stephen Ames, Canada, 67-65–132
Paul Gow, Australia, 68-65–133
Greg Chalmers, Cleveland, Ohio, 67-66–133
Luke Donald, Cleveland, Ohio, 69-64–133
Stuart Appleby, Cleveland, Ohio, 67-66–133
Phil Tataurangi, New Zealand, 70-65–135
Olin Browne, Jupiter, Fla., 65-70–135
Jay Don Blake, St. George, Utah, 67-68–135
Spike McRoy, Huntsville, Ala., 66-69–135
Tim Herron, Golden Valley, Minn., 68-67–135
Steve Haskins, El Paso, Texas, 66-69–135
Donnie Hammond, Lake Mary, Fla., 67-68–135
Woody Austin, Wichita, Kan., 68-68–136
Ben Crane, Minneapolis, Minn., 69-67–136
Steve Pate, Agoura, Calif., 71-65–136
Jim Gallagher Jr., Greenwood, Miss., 70-66–136
George McNeill, Ft. Myers, Fla., 67-69–136
Brad Lardon, Austin, Texas, 69-67–136
Hidemichi Tanaka, Troy, Mich., 65-72–137
Charles Howell, Oklahoma City, Okla., 73-64–137
Brent Geiberger, Palm Desert, Calif., 69-68–137
Jerry Haas, Winston-Salem, N.C., 70-67–137

Kent Jones, Albuquerque, N.M., 66-71–137
Franklin Langham, Peachtree City, Ga., 68-69–137
Michael Clark, Cleveland, Ohio, 69-68–137
Heath Slocum, Pensacola, Fla., 66-71–137
Lucas Glover, Greenville, S.C., 73-64–137
Craig Bowden, Bloomington, Ind., 67-70–137
Brian Gay, Washington, D.C., 69-68–137
(P)Michael Muehr, Cleveland, Ohio, 67-71–138

The Reserve Vineyards and Golf Club (Cupp Course)
Aloha, Ore.
17 players for 1 qualifying spot
Ryan Moore, Puyallup, Wash., 69-69–138

Biltmore Country Club
North Barrington, Ill.
37 players for 2 qualifying spots
Tom Gillis, Lake Orion, Mich., 67-70–137
Adam Spears, Canada, 70-71–141

Derek Tolan

Ian Leggatt

TPC at River's Bend
Cincinnati, Ohio
48 players for 3 qualifying spots
Todd Rose, Fresno, Calif., 67-66–133
Ian Leggatt, Scottsdale, Ariz., 66-68–134
Steve Flesch, Union, Ky., 64-71–135

Old Memorial Golf Club
Tampa, Fla.
77 players for 4 qualifying spots
Greg Norman, Jupiter, Fla., 68-71–139
John Huston, Clearwater, Fla., 68-72–140
*Kevin Warrick, Valrico, Fla., 71-69–140
(P)Tony Soerries, Hobe Sound, Fla., 72-70–142

Ansley Golf Club's Settindown Creek
Atlanta, Ga.
41 players for 3 qualifying spots
Scott Parel, Augusta, Ga., 66-66–132
Thomas Levet, France, 69-70–139
Ken Duke, Boca Raton, Fla., 72-69–141

2002 U.S. Open by the Numbers

Entries – 8,468

Local Qualifying Sites – 105 (May 6-21)
Golfers in Local Qualifying – 8,196
Number Who Advance – 564

Number Who Advance – 564
Golfers Exempt from Local Qualifying – 208
Golfers in Sectional Qualifying – 772

Sectional Qualifying Sites – 12 (June 3-4)
Golfers in Sectional Qualifying – 772
Number Who Advance – 82

Number Who Advance – 82
Golfers Who Were Fully Exempt – 74
Total Golfers in the Championship – 156 (June 13-16)

Boone Valley Golf Club

St. Louis, Mo.

35 players for 3 qualifying spots
Trevor Dodds, St. Louis, Mo., 70-69–139
Mario Tiziani, Chanhassen, Minn., 70-69–139
(P)Tom Pernice Jr., Murrieta, Calif., 72-69–141

Century Country Club and Brae Burn Country Club

Purchase, N.Y.

153 players for 23 qualifying spots
Tom Byrum, Richmond, Texas, 69-69–138
Jean Van de Velde, Geneva, 69-71–140
Jeff Maggert, The Woodlands, Texas, 71-69–140
Jeev Milkha Singh, Edgewater, N.J., 69-72–141
Jay Haas, Reston, Va., 71-70–141
Paul Stankowski, Flower Mound, Texas, 70-71–141
Kelly Gibson, New Orleans, La., 72-69–141
Taichiro Kiyota, Japan, 68-73–141
Pat Perez, Scottsdale, Ariz., 71-70–141
Jason Caron, Jupiter, Fla., 74-68–142
Craig Stadler, Reston, Va., 73-69–142
James McGovern, Oradell, N.J., 69-73–142
Bob Tway, Edmond, Okla., 72-70–142

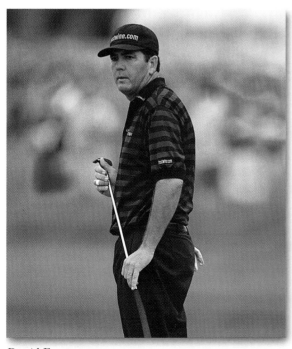

David Frost

Jean Van de Velde

David Frost, Dallas, Texas, 71-71–142
Scott Dunlap, Duluth, Ga., 73-70–143
Kaname Yokoo, Apache Junction, Ariz., 72-71–143
K.J. Choi, Cleveland, Ohio, 70-73–143
Darrell Kestner, Glen Cove, N.Y., 73-70–143
Per-Ulrik Johansson, Tequesta, Fla., 71-73–144
Wayne Grady, Australia, 71-73–144
Harrison Frazar, Dallas, Texas, 72-72–144
Jimmy Carter, Scottsdale, Ariz., 74-70–144
(P)John Maginnes, Greensboro, N.C., 74-70–144

Westmoreland Country Club

Export, Pa.

25 players for 1 qualifying spot
Charles Raulerson Jr., Atlantic Beach, Fla., 67-68–135

Shadow Hawk Club

Houston, Texas

35 players for 2 qualifying spots
Jimmy Walker, Cibolo, Texas, 68-71–139
Andy Sanders, Houston, Texas, 67-72–139

*Denotes amateur   (P) Won playoff

102nd
U.S. OPEN
First Round

At 4:52 on Thursday afternoon, Tiger Woods holed a putt from 10 feet at the second hole at Bethpage State Park's Black Course and grabbed the lead in the 102nd United States Open Championship. Since he began his day from the 10th tee, this was his 11th hole of the round, his fourth birdie and, at three under par, his first clear lead. He would go on to shoot 67 — three under par — on a penal course that punished every mistake and asked for maximum effort on every shot.

At the end of the day, Woods led the young Spaniard Sergio Garcia by one stroke. Only four others in an elite field of 156 of the game's best players broke par 70. Jeff Maggert, Billy Mayfair, Dudley Hart and the Korean K.J. Choi shot 69s.

This was a signal day in the Open's history. It was the first time since its beginning in 1895 that the championship was played over a municipal course, and it was the first time the starting field had been split, with half beginning from the first tee, half from the 10th. The USGA had gone to two tees once before, though, but under unusual circumstances. When heavy rains and a blocked culvert flooded Oak Hill Country Club's East Course in 1989 — ducks actually swam along the sixth fairway — the third-round field played from two tees starting at 1 p.m. Everyone finished, but only the 71 men who had survived the 36-hole cut played.

Plagued by bad weather the last few years, which caused rounds to carry over into the following day, combined with the progressively slowing pace of a field heavily weighted with PGA Tour players, the USGA felt starting from two tees the first two days

might assure the round would finish the same day it started. It worked.

As if this wasn't innovation enough, taking the national championship to a municipal course, one that anyone can plunk down his money and play, seemed revolutionary. That worked as well, principally because Bethpage Black was no ordinary public course.

After a few preliminary practice rounds, Woods called the Black the hardest par 70 he had ever played. Others believed it the hardest course they had played of any denomination.

When the round opened, it looked for a time as if Woods had spoken out of turn. With balls flying into the hole from unlikely spots and players ignoring the Black's perils, Shingo Katayama dipped two under par after six holes, Jim Carter birdied two of his first five and so did Jean Van de Velde. Nick Faldo rolled in a monster putt and birdied the 10th, his opening hole, and apparently trapped in tangled rough at the fourth, Justin Leonard lofted a pitch that dropped into the hole without touching the green for an eagle 3. John Huston holed a pitch at the first, and John Maginnes holed from a bunker.

Those liberties didn't last. At the end of the first round, fewer than half the field had shot under 75, and 15 men didn't break 80. These were not field-fillers. Tom Kite, the 1992 Open champion, shot 80; Hale Irwin, who had won three Opens, shot 82; Wayne Grady, the 1990 PGA champion, shot 84; Bob Estes, the Kemper Insurance Open winner two weeks earlier, shot 81; and Paul Goydos, Joe Durant, Jay Haas and Steve Pate shot in the 80s as well.

More than a few others staggered off Bethpage

Sergio Garcia (68), one stroke off the lead, grimaced as his putt for birdie at the 13th grazed the hole.

First Round

Tiger Woods	67	-3
Sergio Garcia	68	-2
Jeff Maggert	69	-1
K.J. Choi	69	-1
Billy Mayfair	69	-1
Dudley Hart	69	-1
Padraig Harrington	70	E
Franklin Langham	70	E
Stewart Cink	70	E
Phil Michelson	70	E
Nick Faldo	70	E
Steve Lowery	70	E

with bruised egos. The premier grouping of the day sent Retief Goosen, the defending Open champion, off with David Toms, the current PGA champion, and David Duval, the British Open champion. It wasn't pretty. With birdies at the first two holes, Toms went out in 34, but he slumped back in 40 and shot 74, the lowest score of the group. Duval and Goosen played shoddy golf. Duval shot 78 and Goosen 79. After one round, they had little hope of surviving the 36-hole cut.

Everyone struggled on this unyielding course.

Paul Goydos (80) had the honor at 7:15 off the first tee.

Jeff Maggert (69) had struggled all year.

Tiger Woods (67) took what seemed like half of the more than 40,000 spectators with him.

It demanded long and accurate driving, long and precise irons, superb putting and the resignation to deal with deep and dense rough and unusually fast and puzzling greens. Then there was that physically draining slog up and down hilly ground through the early holes, which must have cost some of them leg cramps.

It is unlikely, though, that fatigue caused such high scoring. Put simply, Bethpage would probably rank as the toughest course anyone saw in 2002, even in the benign conditions of the opening day.

Rain had fallen overnight, softening the greens, and play opened Thursday under overcast skies and dropping temperatures, and only a light wind ruffled the leaves on the forest of tall hardwood trees. Temperatures had been high early in the week, but readings dropped into the 60s, cool enough for a number of players to wear sweater vests and for Davis Love III to play in a light-blue rain jacket.

K.J. Choi (69) overcame three consecutive bogeys.

Billy Mayfair (69) posted two birdies.

The New York crowd came in large numbers and let their voices be heard.

Dudley Hart (69) missed three fairways.

Threatening skies had no effect on the galleries. Fans had been pouring through the gates since early morning, swarming over the course, commandeering seats in the grandstands and lining the fairway ropes, waiting for their heroes — or someone to harass. These were not the polite, sedate, genteel galleries of earlier times. These fans came to cheer, to shout "In the hole," to moan when it missed. They whooped, they yelled and sometimes let a player know they knew he had hit a sloppy shot.

They followed John Daly and gasped at his monstrous drives. They followed Greg Norman, hoping he would find his old flair and run up a few birdies. And some, who like to watch golf the way it can be played, watched Faldo, who did indeed revive memories of a lost decade.

Faldo turned 45 a month after the Open, but he seemed much younger. He walked with his old assurance, and he hit the shots he hit when he was winning three British Opens and three Masters Tournaments. With Fanny Sunesson again toting his bag, as she had during his glory years, Faldo played exceptionally steady golf. After his opening birdie at the 10th with a putt of about 40 feet, as long as any holed that day, Faldo birdied the 13th and the ninth, his last hole of the round, from 25 feet, but he rang up 12 pars with the impeccable monotony of old times. With three bogeys, he shot even par, putting himself in the thick of the battle, where he had thrived.

Daly played almost as well, although more erratically. Even though he lost four strokes to par at his first two holes, the 10th and 11th, his gallery hung with him, just to watch him wrap the club around his neck and whip it through the ball.

Starts like that had often wrecked Daly, but here he stuck with it, played the rest of the second nine in even par and moved to the first tee four over, at 39. He had birdied the 18th, then began his homeward nine with birdies at the first and second — three straight birdies. Only two over par now, Daly lost both strokes over the next seven holes, but he played the first nine in 35 and finished the day with 74, not bad after such a wretched start.

Norman had turned 47 in February and, unlike Faldo, who had been given a special exemption, he had to play his way in through a 36-hole qualifying round. While his fans cheered him on, Norman gave them a good show. His blond hair flowing from under his broad-brimmed hat and flashing his engaging smile, he shot a respectable 75, not bad for someone who so seldom entered the wars.

Others expected to play especially well had hard times. Ernie Els, who had tied for second at Pebble Beach two years earlier, shot a dull 73, and Vijay Singh, winner of both a Masters and a PGA Championship, who had finished in the top 10 in the last three Opens, blundered out in 41 but came back in 34 and shot 75, the same score as Mark Brooks, the loser to Goosen in the 2001 playoff.

Jean Van de Velde, of the elegant swing, shot a very decent 71, but Colin Montgomerie birdied only one hole and shot 75.

The early excitement centered around Davis Love III, who had enjoyed his moment of glory at Winged Foot, across Long Island Sound in Mamaroneck, N.Y., where he won the 1997 PGA Championship.

Jose Maria Olazabal (71) had six bogeys on his card.

Love started from the first tee just after 8 a.m., and for a time looked as if he might run away with the championship. While he dropped a stroke at the first, one of Bethpage's easier holes, he steadied himself and played the next three holes in par. Then he showed that Bethpage could be beaten.

Beginning at the fifth, Love ran off five straight 3s, only one of them a par, by holing a string of putts from the 15- to 20-foot range.

Out in 32, in front at three under par, Love lost his touch coming back and shot 39. Truthfully, he should have done better, but two bad breaks cost him strokes. After bogeying the 10th, he played a lovely pitch to the 11th that carried past the hole, braked and spun back toward the hole. It slowed as it approached hole-high, but there it picked up speed and ran off the green. He bogeyed. Two strokes were gone, and he was back to one under.

Then after two fine shots into the 15th, his birdie putt missed the hole to the right, almost

Charles Howell III (71) started and ended with bogeys.

stopped, but caught another slope and ran yards away. Another bogey, and Love had to take 71.

Meanwhile, Garcia was playing steady, forceful golf. Just 22 years old, Garcia may be irritating with his repeated gripping and re-gripping, but he can play wonderful golf.

Off the first tee at 7:45, he slipped two under par quickly, pitching close to the hole for a simple birdie at the fourth, then playing an 8-iron into the fifth and holing a nice putt for another. Two under now, Garcia gave the stroke away by bunkering his approach to the sixth and missing from 12 feet.

Out in 34, he picked up his lost stroke at the 12th, flying a 6-iron onto the green and holing another good putt. He might have birdied the 13th, but his putt grazed the left edge of the hole and ran past. He missed another at the 15th, then saved pars after missing both the 16th and 17th greens. A delicate putt eased into the hole at the 16th, and he holed from 10 feet after bunkering his tee shot to the 17th. He was in with 68, the best of the morning shift.

At about the same time as Garcia, Phil Mickelson had started from the 10th and for a time looked as if he too might make nothing but birdies. His ball-striking couldn't have been better when he nearly holed a stunning 3-iron into the 10th that

David Toms (74) dropped shots at the last two holes.

Scott Hoch (71) was in his 16th consecutive U.S. Open.

pulled up a foot or so from the hole. Then he holed a curling 18-foot putt from the edge of the 11th green for another.

That was two holes played, two under par. Mickelson played the next 16 holes in two over par, finishing with 70, even par. The 15th ruined what had begun as a promising round. Trying to hold a difficult fairway by playing a fade, he let the ball slip into the rough. Two more shots got him to the green, but there he three-putted from 60 feet. He had lost two strokes on one hole.

With 35 on the second nine, he moved over to the first nine, dropped a stroke at the third hole, a difficult par 3, but made up for it by playing another first-class 3-iron to 12 feet and birdieing the eighth, one of only six that day.

More than 40,000 fans held tickets for the Open, and it seemed as if by 1:35 p.m. half had worked their way to the 10th tee, where Woods was to begin his round. When he stepped onto the tee, a great roar thundered through the trees. The gallery rushed to him, jostling one another for position and crowding along the fairway ropes six and seven deep. Most of them saw nothing more than the back of the head of the person in front of them. It didn't seem to matter. They were happy just to be nearby.

Woods left the tee knowing what he had to shoot and he set about doing it. Playing with absolute confidence in his swing and in himself, he moved to the top. He eased past his first three holes, picked up a birdie at the 13th, holing from 18 feet, and added another at the short 14th, holing a 15-footer with a right-to-left break. It ran squarely into the hole.

A stroke slipped away at the 16th, where a wild drive flew so far right it carried beyond the gallery and glanced off a spectator's shoulder. No harm done, it was just a temporary setback. Woods won it back at the 18th by holing from 20 feet after another drive had caught the rough.

With 33 on the second nine, he moved to the

Vijay Singh (75) went out in 41 strokes.

Jesper Parnevik (72) shot 38 and 34.

first tee and played the first nine in 34, with birdies at the second and ninth and a lone bogey at the sixth.

Once again Woods had shown command of his game, using accurate driving, inspired iron play and deadly putting to separate himself from the field. From the tees he hit 11 of the 14 fairways on driving holes, and then hit 13 greens.

Just as he had at Pebble Beach in the first round of the 2002 Open, Woods saved pars at three of the five holes where he missed greens by holing some nerve-wracking putts — from eight feet at the 17th, his eighth hole of the day, from 10 feet at the first and from 12 feet at the seventh. Putting like this demoralizes the other players.

But that is his game. He had squeezed three strokes from a punishing course and challenged the rest of the field to catch him.

It may have been the shot of the week as Tiger Woods (135) played a remarkable pitch to save par at the 17th.

102nd
U.S. OPEN
Second Round

As he stepped off the last green Thursday afternoon, smarting after a round of 79, John Maginnes noted that since Bethpage Black is a public course, fans were calling this U.S. Open "The People's Open."

"Well," he said, "the people must be mad."

If they were angry Thursday, they must have been furious Friday, the day of the second round. Playing through a mentally and physically exasperating combination of rain, soggy fairways, slick greens, unforgiving rough and all-around misery, a field of the game's leading players averaged a surprisingly high 76 strokes against a par of 70.

For all but a few of the more determined, the rain turned an already difficult course into a brutal challenge. On a course that called for long carries to reach some fairways, not everyone had enough length; their drives sank into escape-proof rough. Greens already fast seemed even faster.

The day drove some to claim play should have been stopped during the afternoon, when water collected on greens and tees and a large stream formed on the 18th fairway. Groundsworkers rushed to trouble spots and with their squeegees swept puddles from both tees and greens. The rules could handle casual water on other parts of the course.

Asked how bad it was, Bernhard Langer said, "As bad as can be. Ten on a scale of 10." Langer shot 76.

Scott McCarron shot 72 and said it felt more like 67 on what he called a normal course.

"Anybody who shoots one under, that's like shooting 63 or 64. If you hit it in the rough, you just can't advance it anywhere. The ball was going 15 to 20 yards less than it did yesterday. The course played like 8,000 yards today."

After a disappointing 78, Scott Verplank could say only, "Well, when you have a course with nine par 5s …"

Nick Faldo, who had 76, wasn't overly amused either.

"I had to remind myself I am a golfer. This is golf," Faldo said. "This isn't hiking in a jungle. A machete would have been very useful today. Or a grenade launcher, if I could fire it straight."

After shooting 157 (75 and 82) for the two rounds, Paul Azinger said he was happy not to come back, and Sergio Garcia was obviously upset after 74. He had played through the worst of the weather during the afternoon and seemed peeved because Tiger Woods had gone off early and finished by 2 p.m., in marginally better conditions.

Asked if he felt the USGA should have called off play for the day, Garcia said, "I certainly did," and then went a giant step further. Letting his frustration override his common sense, he went on, "I don't know if Tiger Woods had been out there, I think it would have been called."

Told of Garcia's charge, Tom Meeks smiled and said, "I can assure you that is not true."

As director of rules and competitions for the USGA, Meeks and Fred Ridley, chairman of the championship committee, oversee the Open. They admitted later that they had come close to suspending play when water collected near the hole on the 17th, but the grounds crews swept it away and play continued.

Besides, the greens had held up remarkably well, and so long as the greens were puttable, the Open would go on.

Padraig Harrington (138) made sure his caddie backed away before putting.

the 60s, played in the afternoon. Only Woods teed off with the early shift.

Contradicting Garcia, Dudley Hart felt the wet conditions set up opportunities.

"It makes fairways wider," he said, because, "If it rains and the fairways are soft, the ball doesn't run away and you don't bounce into the rough."

Hart added that when the greens soften, "You might be able to get the ball to back up, which isn't typical of U.S. Open greens."

Phil Mickelson felt much the same, saying, "The course is playing as susceptible [sic] as it can possibly play. If the greens were to be firm and the wind up, like I've seen it in practice rounds, it would be much more difficult. The greens are so perfect that if you start the ball on line, you'll hole the putt."

None of the controversy, charges of favoritism and tales of horror had any effect on Maruyama, the life of every party. Short, squat, powerful and effervescent, to Maruyama a round of golf is total joy; nobody has so much fun. As soon as he steps onto a golf course he beams. When he hits a good shot he beams brighter. When he makes a hole-in-one, he reacts like a kid with a new toy.

Maruyama holed an 8-iron shot on Bethpage's 161-yard 14th. When his ball dived into the hole, Maruyama lofted his hands straight up, leaped up and down and of course beamed. He had just scored his third ace and what is believed to be the 35th hole-in-one ever hit in the Open.

That shot spurred him to a round of 67, the best of the day and a round he called the best he ever played. With it he jumped 89 places, from a tie

Garcia insisted, though, that heavier afternoon weather added three or four strokes to course difficulty. The scores didn't back him up. Morning starters averaged 76.87 strokes per round while those who played in the afternoon averaged 76.09 strokes.

Then, Maginnes, Padraig Harrington and Shigeki Maruyama, three of the four men who shot in

Shigeki Maruyama (143) shot 67 for the day's low round.

for 96th to a tie for seventh. With his opening 76, he had 143 for 36 holes, eight strokes behind Woods, the leader at 135 following a solid 68.

Lost in the frenzy over the ace, Maruyama followed up with a birdie 3 at the 15th, the only birdie that vicious hole surrendered that day. Until his hole-in-one at the 14th and the birdie at the 15th, Maruyama had flirted with missing the cut. Six over after the first round, he had played the first nine in 34, picking up one stroke, but bogeyed both the 10th and 12th. He was seven over now, with all those hard holes ahead.

Maruyama birdied the 13th, aced the 14th and birdied the 15th, a pick-up of four strokes in three holes. Now he had worked back to three over par, certain to survive for the last two rounds. Could he do even better?

Asked if he liked his chances of catching Woods, Maruyama said, through an interpreter, "What are you talking about?"

Under these miserable conditions, players with no better than decent scores made giant leaps. Pad-

raig Harrington climbed from a tie for seventh to second place, at 138, with his own 68. K.J. Choi held on to a share of third place despite shooting 73, four strokes worse than his opening 69.

With a second 71, Davis Love III climbed from a tie for 13th into a tie for third with Choi, Garcia and Jeff Maggert. Heckled by fans irritated with his re-gripping routine, Garcia shot 74, and Maggert shot 73. Ordinarily, with scores like those, they would have dropped dramatically in the standings.

Davis Love III missed the fairway for bogey at the fifth.

Still, with 73, Mickelson held steady in a tie for seventh, where he had begun the day, joined by Maruyama, who had climbed up, and Billy Mayfair, who had fallen back with his 74.

Others didn't play nearly so well. Both Stewart Cink, who missed the 2001 playoff by one stroke, and Steve Lowery followed their opening 70s with 82s and missed the cut.

Then there was Woods. Despite the difficult

Sergio Garcia (142) drove into a bunker at the fifth.

Second Round

Tiger Woods	67 - 68	– 135	-5
Padraig Harrington	70 - 68	– 138	-2
K.J. Choi	69 - 73	– 142	+2
Davis Love III	71 - 71	– 142	+2
Sergio Garcia	68 - 74	– 142	+2
Jeff Maggert	69 - 73	– 142	+2
Billy Mayfair	69 - 74	– 143	+3
Phil Mickelson	70 - 73	– 143	+3
Shigeki Maruyama	76 - 67	– 143	+3

conditions and a few capricious shots, he scored only one stroke higher than his first-round 67. Grouped with the burly Irishman Darren Clarke and Chris DiMarco, who claimed he went through four gloves and three towels that day, Woods ignored the conditions. Instead of moaning, he attacked.

Woods hit a drive past the corner of the dogleg at the first hole, then a wedge to three feet for a birdie. He had an 8-iron to three feet at the uphill second green for another birdie. After a simple par at the third, Woods had two shots and a pitch to eight feet and still another birdie at the difficult fourth for three birdies in four holes. The game was on.

He made routine pars through the seventh, then buried his tee shot under the lip of a bunker at the eighth, the second of Bethpage's four par-3 holes. With hope of saving par depending on a miracle shot, Woods did what he could to avoid making a 5. He chopped the ball from the sand and two-putted for a bogey 4.

A loose drive from the ninth tee, but a lucky break. His ball glanced off a spectator's umbrella, deflecting it to the rough. It was such luck it prompted speculation that, like Daniel Webster, he had made a pact with the devil.

His approach dived into another bunker, he pitched out to 15 feet and, of course, holed the putt. He was out in 33 with the vicious second nine still ahead.

A big gallery stood waiting for Woods at the 10th. One fan called, "Now we separate the men

K.J. Choi (142) got his only birdie at the par-5 fourth.

Phil Mickelson (143) said scores could have been lower.

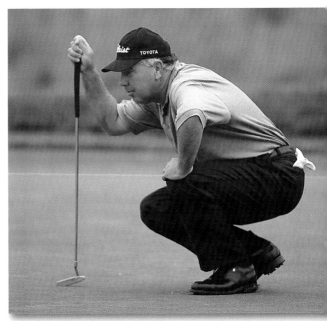

Mark O'Meara (146) recovered after a first-round 76.

from the boys." They swarmed around him, crushing one another against the fairway ropes just for a glimpse.

Bunkered again at the 10th, Woods bogeyed, then ran off four routine pars and bunkered another approach at the 15th. There he holed from 12 feet for another saving putt.

Another routine par at the 16th, but then he played the shot of the championship.

From a downhill lie in deep rough behind the 17th green, with the green falling away, Woods played a remarkable little pitch. It cleared the heavy grass, caught the collar of the green, then began a slow but steady run toward the hole. For a heart-stopping instant it looked as if it certainly would fall for a birdie 2. Instead, it barely skirted the rim and died perhaps two feet past. Woods rolled it in for the par.

His pitch had been a stunning display of touch, nerves and confidence.

He finished with a birdie 3 at the home hole and walked off with his 68, the only man with two rounds under par.

The rain and soggy conditions had had no visible effect on Woods. He had kept his concentration, thought only of the shots he had to play and

Ernie Els (147) was two over on the par 5s.

39

John Daly (150) qualified with 35 on his last nine.

Retief Goosen (154) made an unwanted departure.

made only one concession to the weather. When droplets fell from the bill of his baseball cap, Woods simply wore it backwards, *a la* Ken Griffey Jr. and lots of other mimics.

Why hadn't the rain bothered him?

"Growing up in Southern California, obviously we didn't get a whole lot of rain," Woods said. "When we did, I used to love to go out and play in it. The only hard part was trying to convince my Mom I could go out and play and not catch a cold. That was not easy. I had to do a lot of convincing."

At the time he finished, Woods stood five strokes ahead of the field, but Harrington had been playing just half an hour. By the time he finished, he had cut two strokes from Woods's margin.

Starting from the 10th tee, Harrington drove into the rough, bunkered his approach, pitched out to 12 feet, missed the putt and bogeyed. Defying all reason, this was his only bogey of the day. Like Woods, Harrington refused to let the weather ruin his day.

"I had my head down and was working away, and basically wasn't distracted by the weather," Harrington said. "I was never looking for the round to be suspended."

Harrington scraped out a par after missing both the fairway and the green of the 12th, which saw more bogeys than pars, birdied the short 14th and shot 35. Moving to the first nine, he ran off three pars and birdied the fourth, the only par-5 hole within memory with an average score above par.

One under now, Harrington birdied the sixth as well, shot 33 and 68, and took over as chief challenger to Woods with a total of 138 to Woods's 135.

Harrington's short game and putting had saved his round, for on a day when shots from rough grass could tear the club from your hands, he had hit 10 of the 14 fairways and 11 greens. At the same time, he had one-putted half the holes.

Woods himself had hit just nine fairways, but he had reached 12 greens in regulation figures and, like Harrington, had one-putted nine greens. They would be paired together for the third round.

Meantime, it was time to say farewell to those who missed the 36-hole cut, unusually high at 150, the highest since 1986 at Shinnecock Hills, just a

David Duval (151) said the greens were fast.

Colin Montgomerie (151) left smiling with the crowds.

few miles farther east on Long Island.

High as it was it caught Retief Goosen, the defending Open champion, and David Duval, who had played glorious golf in winning the 2001 British Open. Goosen shot 79-75–154 and Duval 78-73–151, missing by one stroke. Tom Kite, Lee Janzen, Hale Irwin and Steve Jones, former U.S. Open champions, all failed to survive, along with Colin Montgomerie, Mark Calcavecchia, the 1989 British Open champion, Mark Brooks, runner-up in the 2001 U.S. Open, and Wayne Grady, the 1990 PGA champion.

The 16-year-old amateur Derek Tolan, who had won his place in a qualifying round, shot a reasonable 78 in his first round but wore out in the second round and shot 88.

Phil Mickelson (210) shot 67 to match his best-ever score in the U.S. Open, and was five strokes behind.

While overcast skies blocked the sun and the temperature fell to the high 50s Saturday morning, the competitive climate turned warm as the 72-man field played through the U.S. Open's third round. Helped by some loose golf by Tiger Woods, the halfway leader, the championship turned into a tight battle for a time. Then Woods rallied and took command once again.

Missing fairways and leaving approaches too far from the hole for reasonable birdie putts, Woods played the first 14 holes in two over par. Then, facing the challenge, he responded by birdieing both the 15th and 17th and finished in even-par 70. With a 54-hole score of 205, five under par, he opened his lead from three strokes to four.

It had been quite a day. While Woods stuttered, Phil Mickelson climbed from 10 strokes behind to within two. But Woods rallied, Mickelson dropped a stroke, shot 67 and at day's end trailed by five. Sergio Garcia bounced back from his second-round 74, shot 67 as well and moved into second place at 209. Jeff Maggert shot 68 and tied Mickelson at 210.

Billy Mayfair ran off three birdies on the first six holes and shot 68 and 211. Meantime, finding neither fairways nor greens, Padraig Harrington shot 73 and fell from second into a tie for fifth alongside Mayfair and the Australian Robert Allenby, who shot 67. Harrington had begun the day just three strokes behind Woods but now stood six behind.

Reminding the gallery that he had been quite a golfer a decade ago, 44-year-old Nick Faldo shot a precision 66. With 212, he climbed from the depths of 20th place into a tie for eighth with Justin Leo-

nard. Not only was Faldo's 66 the best round of the day, it was the best of the championship and, *ipso facto*, the course record for the new Bethpage.

With the smaller number of players, scoring improved noticeably. Where the average score had been 76 and fractions in the first two rounds, it dropped to 72 strokes in the third. Where the full field had shot only eight rounds under par 70 through the first two rounds, 13 men scored in the 60s in the third, 16 others shot even par and two more shot 71.

Vijay Singh shot 67 after two grim rounds of 75, just making the cut, and jumped from a tie for 60th place all the way to a tie for 22nd. Leonard and Frank Lickliter shot 68s, and Mark O'Meara, Jesper Parnevik, Nick Price and Steve Stricker shot 69s.

And while nobody was looking, Kevin Sutherland had the hottest finish of them all. A 38-year-old Californian who had won only once in six years on the PGA Tour, Sutherland played the last six holes in 19 strokes, an average of 3.16 strokes per hole. He eagled the 13th, birdied the 14th, parred the 15th, birdied the 16th and finished with pars at the 17th and 18th. He shot 70, and at day's end rested in a tie for 35th place, with 219, doing no harm to anyone.

This was the weekend, and bigger galleries crowded in. Fans had filed past security guards and onto the club grounds since daylight, either looking for grandstand seats, strategic spots where they could watch the golfers play particular holes or following players at random. Being selective, others waited for the leading pair to tee off, although Woods and Harrington, the last off, wouldn't begin until nearly 3 p.m.

Sergio Garcia (209), playing here onto the fifth green, posted 67 and regained much of his crowd support.

After Friday's all-day rain, Bethpage was not a pretty sight. The course itself was fine, but beyond the ropes the galleries had churned the ground to soupy sludge. Picking their way gingerly over the wet ground, fans slid and slithered along and occasionally slipped and fell. Most of them came away relatively unhurt, except for their dignity and the prospect of a hefty cleaning bill. Others weren't so lucky; by early afternoon, nearby ambulances had answered four calls to treat the more seriously injured.

The mud rarely affected a golf shot, but when Davis Love's tee shot carried over the third green and rolled down a grassy slope, it probably would have stopped under ordinary conditions. Instead, when it reached a muddy track worn bare by spectator traffic, it rolled yards farther, leaving him a difficult recovery. With a curious gallery clustered around him, he managed it nicely and walked away with a bogey 4 when it might have been worse.

Once again the fans had come to make themselves heard. They yelled and, as usual, bellowed, "In the hole." Listening to the crowd, one spectator remarked, "This is almost like a Mets-Yankees game."

Some of the comments weren't friendly. John Maginnes had worn a rather unusual shirt. As a putt lipped out, someone snarled, "It must be the shirt." A few spectators, still annoyed by Garcia's charges and his constant regripping, suggested he get a tennis racket, a not-so-subtle reference to Garcia's friendship with Martina Hingis, the former Wimbledon champion, who was walking in his gallery. At times they grew so noisy, caddies pleaded for quiet.

As usual, the biggest galleries followed Woods, but there were so many people it is difficult to imag-

Third Round

Tiger Woods	67 - 68 - 70 – 205	-5
Sergio Garcia	68 - 74 - 67 – 209	-1
Phil Mickelson	70 - 73 - 67 – 210	E
Jeff Maggert	69 - 73 - 68 – 210	E
Robert Allenby	74 - 70 - 67 – 211	+1
Billy Mayfair	69 - 74 - 68 – 211	+1
Padraig Harrington	70 - 68 - 73 – 211	+1
Nick Faldo	70 - 76 - 66 – 212	+2
Justin Leonard	73 - 71 - 68 – 212	+2

ine any of them saw much. They stood rows deep, and if they hadn't planned carefully, they might find they had been caught in bottlenecks with no means of escape.

While he had his share rooting for him, Woods didn't have everyone on his side. A corps of fans had suddenly anointed Mickelson the new gallery dar-

Robert Allenby (211) shot 67 with three bogeys.

Jeff Maggert (210) climbed to a share of third place.

45

Billy Mayfair (211), playing alongside Mickelson, the gallery favorite, shot 68 to hold his own.

ling. Crowds waited for him at every hole, cheering him on.

At first he needed all the help he could get. He pulled his drive into the right rough at the first, couldn't reach the green, chipped poorly and bogeyed. After a routine par at the second, he missed the third green and bogeyed again.

Mickelson recovered one stroke by playing a terrific iron into the par-5 fourth, a blind, uphill shot to a green that sloped from front to back. He had played it so well, his ball settled softly and held. He took two putts for the birdie. Just as quickly, he missed the fifth green and dropped the stroke he had just won. Two over par once again, with three bogeys in five holes. It wasn't looking good. He had begun the round eight strokes behind Woods and now he stood 10 behind. Cheering can't change that.

But Mickelson could. His putting touch came back, his irons flew toward the flagsticks, and his drives split the fairways. Over the next 12 holes he hit every fairway, missed only the 11th green and ran off five birdies, including a 3 at the very difficult 15th.

As he approached the 15th green his gallery chanted, "Phil! Phil! Phil!" When the putt fell, the call changed to, "Beat Tiger. Beat Tiger."

He had indeed cut into Woods's lead. At about the time Mickelson birdied the 15th, Woods, playing four holes behind, bogeyed the 11th and slipped two over par for the day. He had begun five under par and now he had fallen to three under. Mickelson, meanwhile, had started three over, and when he birdied the 17th he stood one under, just two strokes behind. One more birdie and he would be climbing Woods's back.

It didn't happen. His hopes died in the tangled rough of the 18th hole. His drive settled in such deep grass Mickelson had no hope of reaching the

	LEADERS	TODAY	HOLE	TOTAL
	WOODS	1	15	4
	HARRINGTON	2	15	0
	GARCIA	3	17	4
	LOVE	2	16	2
	LEONARD	2	F	2
	MAGGERT	2	17	2
	FALDO	4	F	2
	ALLENBY	3	F	1
	MAYFAIR	2	F	0
	MICKELSON	3	F	0

TODAY	THRU 15	TOTAL
2	HARRINGTON	0
1	TIGER	4

He was the leader by either name.

Padraig Harrington (211) fell six strokes behind.

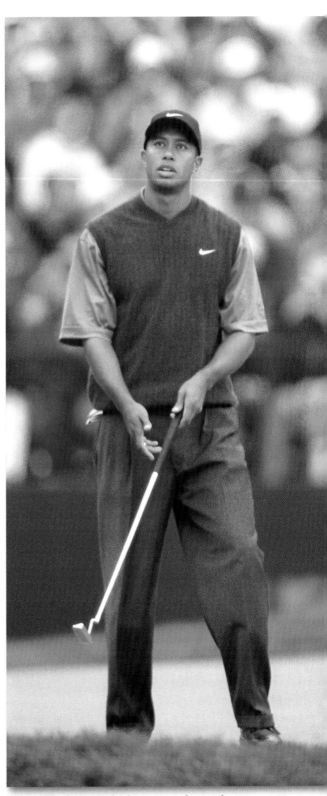

Tiger Woods (205) had a testing day early on.

47

Justin Leonard (212) held a top-10 position.

Nick Faldo (212) had 66, the low round of the week.

Enterprising New Yorkers found prime viewing areas.

green. He closed with a bogey 5 and shot 67. Not only did it match the best round he had ever shot in an Open — he had shot 67 in the first round at Pinehurst in 1999 — until 2001, when he had two, he had scored in the 60s in only three other rounds of his Open career, which dated back to his amateur days in 1990.

Mickelson wasn't alone in nibbling at Woods's lead. Among those closest to him at day's end, both Maggert and Garcia had taken bites from it as well.

Playing together, they teed off 20 minutes ahead of Woods and Harrington, just ahead of Love and K.J. Choi, both of whom lost ground, Love with his 72 and Choi with his second 73.

By Saturday morning, Garcia had recovered from his Friday sulk and evidently regretted he had implied the USGA had given Woods special treatment. He left Woods an apologetic note, and when they passed in the press facility late Saturday, he spoke to him softly and explained about the note. A few of those standing close enough said they saw tears in Garcia's eyes.

Garcia had had a rocky day with the fans as well

and committed a foolish sin by reacting to the heckling. When he heard a chorus counting his pre-shot waggles, chanting in cadence, "Ten! Eleven! Twelve!" Garcia had glared and motioned to the crowd. Some called his gesture obscene.

By Saturday the pique had worn off. The ruder elements still tried to bait him, but Garcia either charmed them with a disarming smile or, when someone bellowed, "Hey, human rain delay," ignored him. On this day Garcia stuck to his golf and won back a few fans.

Both he and Maggert played first-class golf, Garcia with his usual flair, Maggert quietly efficient. Both scrambled. Maggert one-putted six of the first nine greens and three more on the second nine. He had putted remarkably well over the last 36 holes, one-putting nine greens both days, plus holing a chip to save par at the 12th Friday. Garcia did almost as well, one-putting eight greens, just four for birdies.

Not a big man, Maggert stands 5-feet-9 inches and weighs just over 160 pounds, about average. With his simple, compact, effortless-appearing

Tom Byrum (214) birdied two of the last six.

swing, he played a truly remarkable third round. Over a merciless course with unrelenting demands, Maggert played 18 holes without a single bogey. Seven of those nine one-putt greens saved pars and two went for birdies, one on each nine.

He birdied the fourth, where for the first time the field averaged under par, and the 14th, the par 3. He went out in 34 and came back in 34 — a symmetrical 68.

This was Maggert's 12th Open, so he was no stranger. He had finished as high as fourth twice, but he had played rather badly in his last two. He had missed the cut at Pebble Beach in 2000 and tied

Scott McCarron (214) went out in 33.

for 44th at Southern Hills in 2001.

At the age of 22, Garcia was playing in only his third Open. He had never figured at Pebble Beach, but he had played three excellent rounds at Southern Hills and went into the last round in a tie for third place. A fumbling 77 dropped him to a tie for 12th.

Now, at Bethpage, Garcia played his third round more erratically than Maggert. He began with a marvelous pitch to within six feet and birdied the first hole, but he struggled for his par at the second, bunkered his tee shot and bogeyed the third, went for the fourth green on his second shot with a 3-iron and held it, scoring another birdie. Another birdie at the eighth and he had gone out in 33, two under par.

The last group wasn't off until 2:50.

Starting back, he stumbled at the 10th and dropped another stroke, but he picked up birdies at the 14th and the tough 16th, and played the second nine in 34. With 67, he had cut three strokes from par and moved into second place, four strokes behind.

This had been a much better day for Garcia in every respect. It seemed as if by apologizing to Woods he had purged himself of guilt feelings. He smiled a lot and the fans warmed to him, a welcome change because a heroic challenge lay ahead.

Love and Choi had played behind Garcia and had dropped back, but now Woods and Harrington stepped onto the tee a few minutes before 3 p.m. Harrington was never in it and Woods struggled as well. Missing fairways on both opening holes, he still scraped out his pars.

In his day, Jack Nicklaus drove everyone mad by reaching greens from matted rough. Woods is building the same reputation. Even this dense, tortuous grass hadn't stopped him from reaching both the first and second greens, but it caught up with him at the fourth. He drove into the right rough, chopped out across the fairway into the left rough, and his pitch caught the grass a foot or so short of the green. From there he chipped on and saved his par.

Throughout his career, Woods had thrived on par-5 holes, scoring more birdies than pars, but Bethpage's

Davis Love III (214) shot 72 despite making four birdies.

Putting here at the 17th, Woods said later, "I hung in there and was able to make two big putts on 15 and 17."

fourth would not yield to him. He had played it three times now and had birdied it just once. Still, he was even par so far.

Not for long. After a big drive, his approach barely cleared a bunker and stopped short of the fifth green. A loose chip, two putts, and he had the first of his two bogeys.

He made pars through the rest of the first nine, but took a bogey at the 11th, where he missed another green.

By then the scoreboards told him Mickelson, Garcia and Maggert had closed in. Still struggling, Woods missed the 12th green, yet saved par, then wasted two superb shots at the 13th, at 554 yards the longest of the two par 5s. His second shot cleared the yawning bunker guarding the front and held the green. Then he three-putted, his first three-putt green of the week. Instead of a certain birdie, he stalked off with a par, his second on a par-5 hole.

Mickelson had birdied the 17th by then and had climbed within two strokes, and both Garcia and Maggert stood at even par for the distance, just three strokes back. They were putting pressure on Woods.

Now he reacted as all the great players. Woods attacked.

A steady par 3 at the 14th, then a blistering 6-iron into the 15th green to 12 feet, and the putt dropped; his first birdie of the day. A routine par at the next, then another fine 6-iron shot into the 17th and an eight-foot putt for another birdie. With par at the 18th Woods had shot 70 and 205 for the 54 holes, five under par.

Not only had he answered the challenge, he had thrown it back at the challengers. Four strokes ahead now, he had given the rest of the field a lesson. This was *his* Open. If someone wanted it, he would have to take it. Woods wouldn't give it away.

As he stepped onto the first tee at Bethpage Black Sunday afternoon, Tiger Woods held unquestioned command of the 102nd United States Open Championship. First of all, he had the best game anyone had seen in years. Second, he held a four-stroke lead over Sergio Garcia, in second place, and a five-stroke edge over Phil Mickelson and Jeff Maggert. Third, he had established a custom of not losing tournaments he had led this late. In the seven major competitions he had won since 1997, he had either led by himself after three rounds or had been tied for first place.

Furthermore, he had big game in his sights. Two years earlier, in 2000, he had placed fifth in the Masters, then won the U.S. Open, the British Open and the PGA Championship. Eight months later, in April of 2001, he won his second Masters. He held all four trophies, but he hadn't won them in the same year, the standard Bobby Jones had set in 1930 by winning the Open and Amateur championships of the United States and Britain.

Now Woods was hot on the trail of winning all four in 2002. He had won the Masters, and here he stood within one round of winning the U.S. Open. Thirty years had passed since Jack Nicklaus had won both in 1972. He was the fourth, following Craig Wood (1941), Ben Hogan (1951 and 1953) and Arnold Palmer (1960).

Later on the last day, after the carnage of nervous shots, damaging bogeys, lost hopes and vanished dreams had passed, Woods had his second U.S. Open. He shot 72 in the last round, beat off Mickelson's threat, overwhelmed Garcia and won by three strokes. He shot 277 for the 72 holes, three under a brutal par. Only he among the 72 men who played all four rounds had scored under par.

It was only the sixth time, including Woods's victory at Pebble Beach in 2000, that a player had led the U.S. Open from start to finish without being tied at the end of any round. Others who had done it were Walter Hagen (1914), Jim Barnes (1921), Hogan (1953) and Tony Jacklin (1970).

Mickelson closed with 70 and placed second at 280 and Maggert took third place at 282 with his final 72. Garcia fell from second to fourth, at 283, after a fumbling 74 finish. And catching everyone off guard, 46-year-old Scott Hoch climbed from a tie for 17th place into a tie for fifth with an inspired 69, a round sparked by a hole-in-one at the 17th, a 207-yard par 3. Since Hoch had already birdied the 14th, he played both par-3 holes of the second nine in a total of three strokes.

At 285, five over par, Hoch tied with Nick Faldo and Billy Mayfair. Faldo closed with 73 and Mayfair shot 74.

It was a bad day for scoring. After three days of only light breezes, a brisk wind whistled through the trees. With gusts approaching 30 miles an hour, it baffled club selection and mis-directed shots. It turned hard holes even harder, sweeping across some holes, whipping directly into others. Drives at the ninth and 12th became even longer.

The added obstacle of the wind, along with the mental strain of playing for the national championship, sent scores higher. Where 13 men had shot in the 60s in the third round, only Hoch, Stuart Appleby and Peter Lonard scored under 70 in the fourth. Both Appleby and Hoch shot 69s, but Lonard shot 67, the best round of the day.

Appleby finished well behind in a tie for 37th

"This was tough," said Tiger Woods (277). "The conditions were difficult and changing every day."

Billy Mayfair (285) was pleased with a top-10 finish.

Nick Faldo (285) said he struggled in the wind.

place, and Lonard was alone in 11th.

Lonard's round must rank as the most unusual of the week. Even though he bested par by three strokes, he lost three strokes at the 12th and one more at the 16th. Tweaking it a little, he played two holes in four over par and 16 in seven under. Logic tells us somebody could have shot a record score. It was possible.

A Monday finish could have been possible as well. For a time it seemed even probable. Aiming to conclude the Open during prime television viewing time, the final pair of Woods and Garcia teed off at 3:30 in the afternoon, plenty of time to finish in good light at that time of year, assuming all went well. Rain had been forecast, however, and all didn't go well.

Skies had been bright and clear and the sun warm through the morning, but clouds built up in the afternoon, suggesting heavy weather could be closing in. The storm broke just before 6 p.m. Woods and Garcia had finished the 11th hole and up ahead Mickelson had holed out at the 12th but Maggert hadn't.

The rain fell gently at first but pounded heavily within a few minutes, then thunder rolled and sensors detected lightning close by. Just after 6:00, a USGA rules official beside the 13th fairway chanted into his radio, "Five, four, three, two, one, suspend!"

Sirens blared, the gallery broke for shelter, players scurried to waiting vans, and officials huddled.

Within less than an hour the rain let up, the threat of lightning faded, and the players returned. Now it was nearly 7:00, time enough to finish, but this had been a serious loss of time. Another delay and the Open would be held over.

Fortune smiled. The storm blew away and the Open ended on schedule. And while it ended as nearly everyone expected, it had its moments.

Fourth Round

Tiger Woods	67 - 68 - 70 - 72 – 277	-3
Phil Mickelson	70 - 73 - 67 - 70 – 280	E
Jeff Maggert	69 - 73 - 68 - 72 – 282	+2
Sergio Garcia	68 - 74 - 67 - 74 – 283	+3
Scott Hoch	71 - 75 - 70 - 69 – 285	+5
Nick Faldo	70 - 76 - 66 - 73 – 285	+5
Billy Mayfair	69 - 74 - 68 - 74 – 285	+5
Nick Price	72 - 75 - 69 - 70 – 286	+6
Tom Byrum	72 - 72 - 70 - 72 – 286	+6
Padraig Harrington	70 - 68 - 73 - 75 – 286	+6
Peter Lonard	73 - 74 - 73 - 67 – 287	+7

Again the galleries swarmed in, but now they clustered around only those few groups toward the end of the field. As before, they heckled Garcia. After waiting for one of his endless re-gripping routines at the third tee, one fan called, "Take another 20 minutes. Take another half hour."

As he addressed his ball on the fourth fairway, another yelled, "Hit the ball!"

Spotting Martina Hingis in Garcia's gallery at the 10th, a male voice begged, "Hey, Garcia. Hook me up with Kournikova," a reference to the popular tennis star.

All the while they were especially kind to Mickelson. Acknowledging his 32nd birthday Sunday, they sang "Happy Birthday" and urged, "Win it for your birthday. Win it for Father's Day."

Mickelson gave it a game try.

Five strokes behind as he stood on the first tee, he rifled a drive past the point where the fairway swings toward the hole and lofted a sand wedge to the green. He pulled it slightly, but the ball hit a rise, jumped left, rolled past the hole and died within four feet. He holed it. Moments later Woods bogeyed, and now Mickelson stood within three strokes with 17 holes to play.

From the beginning, Woods played loose golf. A timid approach almost backed off the first green, a miserable first putt never once threatened the hole, and he missed the second. After a 2-iron from the second tee and a pitching wedge to the green, he played another nervous putt that broke away from

Peter Lonard (287) shot 67 with seven birdies.

Jay Haas (288) qualified for the 2003 Open.

Jeff Maggert (282) said he "half bladed and half shanked" this shot at the third. He took a double-bogey 5.

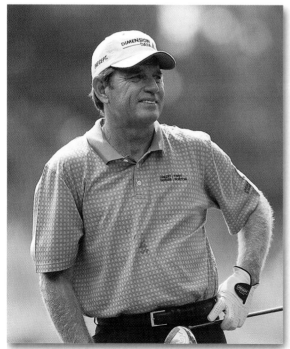

Nick Price (286) shot 70 to tie for eighth place.

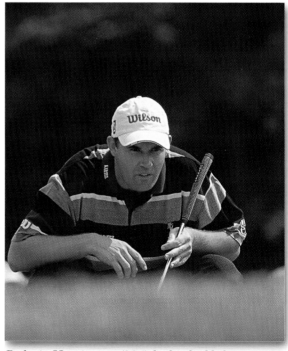

Padraig Harrington (286) had a double bogey at 18.

Phil Mickelson (280) could see only the top of the flagstick at the fourth as he played from near the fifth tee.

the hole and he three-putted again for another bogey. From five under, Woods had fallen back to three under. His lead was shrinking.

While Woods was starting bogey-bogey, Garcia parred both and picked up two strokes. He and Mickelson were tied at one under par, just two strokes behind Woods.

Up ahead everyone else had trouble. Maggert had run off two steady pars, but from the left green-side bunker of the third, he shanked his sand wedge, made five on a par-3 hole, and spent the rest of the day trying to make up the lost ground.

After his third-round 67, Robert Allenby could do nothing right. He bogeyed the first two holes and went out in 38, on his way to 77. Mayfair lost his magic as well, shot his own 38, but came back in 36 for 74. Padraig Harrington had nothing left and shot 75, Justin Leonard shot 76, and Davis Love III moved only backwards, scored a 7 at the fifth and finished with 77. The battle would be among Woods, Mickelson and Garcia.

After his opening birdie, Mickelson lost his edge as well, played some sloppy irons and was lucky to hang on. His pitch to the second flew to the back of the green, he missed the third green, and nobody remembered seeing a ball miss a green so badly as his second shot to the fourth. It drifted left, caught a slope and ran down a steep hill almost to the fifth tee.

Facing a delicate shot, Mickelson threaded a pitch through a narrow alley onto the green, two-putted and saved his par. In his position, though, par wouldn't do. He needed birdies. Instead, he made bogeys.

His 8-iron flew over the fifth green, and he had a poor recovery and two putts for a 5. Then he played a miserable hole. Playing an iron from the sixth tee, he pulled his ball into the high grass, flew it across the fairway into a feet-below-the-ball lie in even higher grass, pitched into a bunker and holed a good putt to save his 5. It was his second bogey. One over par for the day.

A birdie at the 13th gave Mickelson a chance to win.

One hole later, Mickelson recovered one of the lost strokes by holing from about 35 feet at the eighth. He was back to even par for the day, and within three strokes of Woods once again.

Throughout his rocky stretch, Mickelson's fans stood with him. Moments later, when the scoreboard at the ninth green showed his birdie, a pro-Mickelson gallery whistled, yelled, clapped their hands and called his name. They waited for him and cheered when he parred the ninth.

By then Garcia had three-putted the third and dropped one stroke, and when he bogeyed the seventh as well, he was finished. He didn't birdie a hole until the 14th, but it was no help. He had already bogeyed two more holes.

Just as Garcia fell out of the hunt, Woods found his putting stroke, righted his game and birdied the seventh. That was one stroke taken back. He nearly took back another at the ninth, where his putt ducked into the hole and spun out. He made par 4, and was out in 36. His shaky putting aside, Woods had protected his lead by playing steady tee-to-green golf. He had hit every fairway and every green except the fourth and ninth.

Mickelson had driven almost as well, but he had hit only four greens. His putting had saved him. He had one-putted six of the first nine greens, two for birdies, three to save pars and one to salvage a bogey. On to the home nine.

Now his gallery's enthusiasm hit new levels. Riding a quartering wind, Mickelson drilled a drive down the 10th fairway and followed with a terrific iron shot inside 20 feet. His putt grazed the edge of the hole, and he took his par.

He hit another piercing drive to the 11th and a perfectly gauged 9-iron that caught the green and pulled up no more than four feet from the hole.

As the ball settled, fans shouted his name and called, "Go, Phil." It was still noisy as he lined up his putt, but marshals raised their hands and the crowd hushed. Only the drone of a blimp circling overhead broke the stillness as he stroked the putt. When the ball dived into the hole, the crowd's roar strained ear drums. Mickelson had dipped one under par, within range once again.

One hole later, after Mickelson had finished the 12th and Woods and Garcia had completed their 10th, sirens sounded, suspending play.

Within an hour sirens sounded again, the players returned, and the Open resumed. Now Mickelson gave his fans another thrill.

After a big drive at the 13th, the 554-yard par 5, he ripped a high 3-wood shot that carried about 250 yards, cleared the guarding bunker fronting the green and settled on the collar. Two putts and he had another birdie. Mickelson had played his first 42 holes in five over par and his last 25 in seven under. He was still alive.

Mickelson's hopes died at the 16th when, from the rough, he hit into a bunker and took a bogey 5.

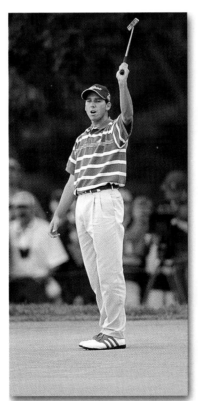

Sergio Garcia (289), who was frustrated with his putt here at the 10th, had only one birdie.

By the time Woods got to the 16th, it did not matter that he hit into a bunker and took a bogey.

From the twilight of the 18th fairway, Woods reached the green and could afford three putts.

Within the next 10 minutes, though, the suspense ended. Woods followed with two glorious shots of his own into the 13th, and his putt nearly fell for an eagle. Another birdie. Five under par now, fairly safe.

The Open ended at the 16th. Mickelson's drive settled on the edge of the rough; his mis-played approach dived into a bunker, and he bogeyed. Even Woods's bogey at the 16th couldn't save him. Then Mickelson took three putts from 20 feet at the 17th for another bogey. Woods had won.

It wasn't a pretty finish, though. Going for a birdie at the 18th, Woods rammed his putt yards past the hole, missed coming back and bogeyed again. He shot 72, his first round over par.

Even with his staggering finish, Woods had beaten Mickelson by three strokes and taken another step toward his Grand Slam.

At the age of 26, Woods had already accomplished more than only a select few had achieved in the game's modern era. This was his second Open. He had already won a British Open, two PGA Championships and three Masters Tournaments.

As dusk settled over Bethpage, as the galleries wandered off, as the players headed for their next stop and as the press composed their accounts of the week's events, an already extraordinary record seemed certain to grow ever more monumental.

Woods now had his second U.S. Open.

Tiger Woods won his eighth USGA national championship, one fewer than the record of Bobby Jones.

102nd
U.S. OPEN
Epilogue

By just about any measure, the 102nd U.S. Open Championship can be judged a success. It was won by Tiger Woods, the best golfer of his generation, it was played over a course that must rank among the most difficult in years, and it was seen probably by more people than any other Open.

Because the Black Course at Bethpage State Park sits among such vast acreage, the USGA allowed more than 40,000 fans to buy tickets. Judging from the size of each day's galleries, every one of them came, a good many during practice rounds early in the week. Monday afternoon, for example, the first day of scheduled practice rounds, fans crowded the Farmingdale platform of the Long Island Rail Road, bussed there from the golf course. Parking wasn't allowed at Bethpage; everyone who came took a shuttle, many from Jones Beach State Park, on Long Island's south shore.

Then there was television. NBC reported a weekend audience of 55 million. No figures were available on foreign viewing, which certainly would account for millions more. It reached every country where golf is played, and perhaps some where it isn't.

The golf course itself stands among the hardest we'll ever see. By measurement it exceeded Congressional Country Club, near Washington, by just one yard, but it played much longer because of other factors. Bethpage demanded very long carries even to reach the fairways, sometimes over 260 yards. In the heavy, humid air of Friday's second round, a few players couldn't reach them, and clearing the crossbunker at the 12th was out of the question. Those who couldn't clear it had scant hope of reaching the green.

Other elements of the course setup — that is tee placement, rough lines and hole locations — weren't universally praised either. Nick Price felt Bethpage, as it played for the Open, eliminated too many players and asked for excessive length.

One other point. The Bethpage Open had been billed as "The People's Open" because Bethpage is a public facility. You pay your money and tee up your ball.

It must be understood, though, that this was not the Bethpage Black the public had played since the middle 1930s. This was a new course, rebuilt over five years and redesigned by Rees Jones, who was given a mandate to create a suitable test to identify the best players in the game.

Woods had won eight of the game's most important competitions by the time he had barely reached the age of having to shave every day. He was only 26 years old. Ordinarily it would be folly to evaluate a man's career at 26, but we must accept that if this young man suddenly walked away from the game, he would have left a Promethean record.

Looking back through golf's history for young men who played better than anyone of their times, as Woods has done, only two names surface — Young Tom Morris and Bobby Jones. Both were true prodigies. Young Tom had won four British Opens before he turned 22, and by 26, Jones had won two U.S. Opens, two British Opens and four U.S. Amateurs. Except for the British Amateur, these were all that were open to him.

Judging from the record Woods has built since he burst into professional golf late in 1996, it appears likely he belongs with them. That he merits standing above them can't be said. But give him time.

102nd
U.S. OPEN
Bethpage State Park

June 13-16, 2002, Bethpage State Park, Black Course, Farmingdale, N.Y.

Contestant	Rounds				Total	Prize
Tiger Woods	67	68	70	72	277	$1,000,000.00
Phil Mickelson	70	73	67	70	280	585,000.00
Jeff Maggert	69	73	68	72	282	362,356.00
Sergio Garcia	68	74	67	74	283	252,546.00
Nick Faldo	70	76	66	73	285	182,882.00
Scott Hoch	71	75	70	69	285	182,882.00
Billy Mayfair	69	74	68	74	285	182,882.00
Tom Byrum	72	72	70	72	286	138,669.00
Padraig Harrington	70	68	73	75	286	138,669.00
Nick Price	72	75	69	70	286	138,669.00
Peter Lonard	73	74	73	67	287	119,357.00
Robert Allenby	74	70	67	77	288	102,338.00
Jay Haas	73	73	70	72	288	102,338.00
Dudley Hart	69	76	70	73	288	102,338.00
Justin Leonard	73	71	68	76	288	102,338.00
Shigeki Maruyama	76	67	73	73	289	86,372.00
Steve Stricker	72	77	69	71	289	86,372.00
Luke Donald	76	72	70	72	290	68,995.00
Steve Flesch	72	72	75	71	290	68,995.00
Charles Howell III	71	74	70	75	290	68,995.00
Thomas Levet	71	77	70	72	290	68,995.00
Mark O'Meara	76	70	69	75	290	68,995.00
Craig Stadler	74	72	70	74	290	68,995.00
Jim Carter	77	73	70	71	291	47,439.00
Darren Clarke	74	74	72	71	291	47,439.00
Chris DiMarco	74	74	72	71	291	47,439.00
Ernie Els	73	74	70	74	291	47,439.00
Davis Love III	71	71	72	77	291	47,439.00
Jeff Sluman	73	73	72	73	291	47,439.00
Jason Caron	75	72	72	73	292	35,639.00
K.J. Choi	69	73	73	77	292	35,639.00
Paul Lawrie	73	73	73	73	292	35,639.00
Scott McCarron	72	72	70	78	292	35,639.00
Vijay Singh	75	75	67	75	292	35,639.00
Shingo Katayama	74	72	74	73	293	31,945.00
Bernhard Langer	72	76	70	75	293	31,945.00
Stuart Appleby	77	73	75	69	294	26,783.00
Thomas Bjorn	71	79	73	71	294	26,783.00
Niclas Fasth	72	72	74	76	294	26,783.00
Donnie Hammond	73	77	71	73	294	26,783.00
Franklin Langham	70	76	74	74	294	26,783.00
Rocco Mediate	72	72	74	76	294	26,783.00
Kevin Sutherland	74	75	70	75	294	26,783.00
Hidemichi Tanaka	73	73	72	76	294	26,783.00
Robert Karlsson	71	76	72	76	295	20,072.00
Tom Lehman	71	76	72	76	295	20,072.00

Contestant	Rounds				Total	Prize
Kenny Perry	74	76	71	74	295	20,072.00
David Toms	74	74	70	77	295	20,072.00
Jean Van de Velde	71	75	74	75	295	20,072.00
Craig Bowden	71	77	74	74	296	16,294.00
Tim Herron	75	74	73	74	296	16,294.00
Frank Lickliter	74	76	68	78	296	16,294.00
Jose Maria Olazabal	71	77	75	73	296	16,294.00
Harrison Frazar	74	73	75	75	297	14,764.00
Ian Leggatt	72	77	72	76	297	14,764.00
Jesper Parnevik	72	76	69	80	297	14,764.00
Corey Pavin	74	75	70	78	297	14,764.00
Brad Lardon	73	73	74	78	298	13,988.00
John Maginnes	79	69	73	78	299	13,493.00
Greg Norman	75	73	74	77	299	13,493.00
Bob Tway	72	78	73	76	299	13,493.00
Andy Miller	76	74	75	75	300	12,794.00
Jeev Milkha Singh	75	75	75	75	300	12,794.00
Paul Stankowski	72	77	77	74	300	12,794.00
Spike McRoy	75	75	74	77	301	12,340.00
Angel Cabrera	73	73	79	77	302	12,000.00
Brad Faxon	75	74	73	80	302	12,000.00
Kent Jones	76	74	74	79	303	11,546.00
Len Mattiace	72	73	78	80	303	11,546.00
John Daly	74	76	81	73	304	11,083.00
Tom Gillis	71	76	78	79	304	11,083.00
*Kevin Warrick	73	76	84	74	307	

Contestant				Contestant				Contestant			
Mark Calcavecchia	74	77	151	Brent Geiberger	75	78	153	Mario Tiziani	76	80	156
John Cook	74	77	151	John Huston	75	78	153	Paul Azinger	75	82	157
Ben Crane	75	76	151	Lee Janzen	76	77	153	Olin Browne	76	81	157
David Duval	78	73	151	Tom Kite	80	73	153	Trevor Dodds	77	80	157
Brian Gay	75	76	151	Scott Verplank	75	78	153	Craig Parry	79	78	157
Lucas Glover	74	77	151	Jimmy Walker	77	76	153	Steve Pate	82	75	157
Steve Haskins	74	77	151	Stephen Ames	77	77	154	Pat Perez	76	81	157
Matt Kuchar	76	75	151	Billy Andrade	72	82	154	Adam Scott	77	80	157
Colin Montgomerie	75	76	151	Jay Don Blake	74	80	154	Kaname Yokoo	78	79	157
Peter O'Malley	75	76	151	Bob Estes	81	73	154	Joe Durant	81	77	158
Tom Pernice Jr.	75	76	151	Kelly Gibson	77	77	154	Matt Gogel	78	80	158
Todd Rose	71	80	151	Retief Goosen	79	75	154	Paul Gow	76	82	158
Kirk Triplett	73	78	151	Steve Jones	74	80	154	Paul Goydos	80	78	158
Stewart Cink	70	82	152	Paul McGinley	75	79	154	Jerry Haas	80	78	158
Jim Gallagher Jr.	75	77	152	James McGovern	75	79	154	George McNeil	79	79	158
Per-Ulrik Johansson	78	74	152	Ben Portie	77	77	154	David Howell	78	81	159
*Taichiro Kiyota	73	79	152	Andy Sanders	77	77	154	Charles Raulerson Jr.	78	81	159
Steve Lowery	70	82	152	Hal Sutton	77	77	154	Tony Soerries	84	76	160
Craig Perks	76	76	152	Woody Austin	79	76	155	Michael Clark	83	80	163
Phil Tataurangi	74	78	152	Michael Campbell	72	83	155	Hale Irwin	82	81	163
Michael Weir	78	74	152	Pete Jordan	76	79	155	Darrell Kestner	77	86	163
*Ricky Barnes	78	75	153	Jerry Kelly	76	79	155	Scott Parel	82	83	165
Mark Brooks	75	78	153	*Ryan Moore	76	79	155	Heath Slocum	83	82	165
Greg Chalmers	72	81	153	Michael Muehr	77	78	155	Adam Speirs	80	85	165
Jose Coceres	77	76	153	Joey Sindelar	76	79	155	*Derek Tolan	78	88	166
Ken Duke	76	77	153	Michael Allen	77	79	156	Wayne Grady	84	83	167
Scott Dunlap	75	78	153	David Frost	75	81	156	Felix Casas	82	92	174
Jim Furyk	73	80	153	Blaine McCallister	77	79	156	Toshimitsu Izawa	80		WD

Professionals not returning 72-hole scores received $1,000 each.

*Denotes amateur.

102nd
U.S. OPEN
Statistics

Hole	1	2	3	4	5	6	7	8	9	10	11	12	13	14	15	16	17	18	Total	
Par	4	4	3	5	4	4	4	3	4	4	4	4	5	3	4	4	3	4	70	
Tiger Woods																				
Round 1	4	(3)	3	5	4	[5]	4	3	(3)	4	4	4	(4)	(2)	4	[5]	3	(3)	67	
Round 2	(3)	(3)	3	(4)	4	4	4	[4]	4	[5]	4	4	5	3	4	4	3	(3)	68	
Round 3	4	4	3	5	[5]	4	4	3	4	4	[5]	4	5	3	(3)	4	(2)	4	70	
Round 4	[5]	[5]	3	5	4	4	(3)	3	4	4	4	4	(4)	3	4	[5]	3	[5]	72	277
Phil Mickelson																				
Round 1	4	4	[4]	5	4	4	4	(2)	4	(3)	(3)	[5]	(4)	3	[6]	4	3	4	70	
Round 2	4	4	3	5	4	[5]	4	3	[5]	[5]	(3)	[5]	5	3	4	4	[4]	(3)	73	
Round 3	[5]	4	[4]	(4)	[5]	4	(3)	(2)	(3)	4	4	4	(4)	3	(3)	4	(2)	[5]	67	
Round 4	(3)	4	3	5	[5]	[5]	4	(2)	4	4	(3)	4	(4)	3	4	[5]	[4]	4	70	280
Jeff Maggert																				
Round 1	(3)	4	3	(4)	[5]	4	4	[4]	(3)	[5]	4	4	(4)	3	4	[5]	3	(3)	69	
Round 2	4	[6]	(2)	5	4	[5]	4	[4]	(3)	[5]	[5]	4	5	(2)	4	4	3	4	73	
Round 3	4	4	3	(4)	4	4	4	3	4	4	4	4	5	(2)	4	4	3	4	68	
Round 4	4	4	[5]	(4)	(3)	4	[5]	3	4	4	4	4	5	3	[5]	4	3	4	72	282

◯ Circled numbers represent birdies or eagles.   ▢ Squared numbers represent bogeys or worse.

Hole	Yards	Par	Eagles	Birdies	Pars	Bogeys	Double Bogeys	Higher	Average
1	430	4	0	40	275	123	16	1	4.259
2	389	4	0	56	268	113	18	0	4.204
3	205	3	1	46	279	117	9	3	3.211
4	517	5	2	109	245	82	15	2	5.011
5	451	4	0	32	235	157	26	5	4.422
6	408	4	0	46	289	106	11	3	4.202
7	489	4	0	23	222	182	25	3	4.479
8	210	3	0	18	287	133	14	3	3.334
9	418	4	0	66	295	83	11	0	4.086
OUT	3,517	35	3	436	2,395	1,096	145	20	37.208
10	492	4	0	22	215	187	31	0	4.499
11	435	4	0	31	259	132	29	4	4.376
12	499	4	0	22	214	187	25	7	4.523
13	554	5	2	116	257	69	9	2	4.941
14	161	3	1	100	302	46	6	0	2.903
15	459	4	0	28	188	186	44	9	4.600
16	479	4	0	39	222	165	27	2	4.411
17	207	3	1	41	285	112	15	1	3.224
18	411	4	1	62	256	113	20	3	4.220
IN	3,697	35	5	461	2,198	1,197	206	28	37.697
TOTAL	7,214	70	8	897	4,593	2,293	351	48	74.905

Date	Winner	Score	Runner-Up	Venue
1895	Horace Rawlins	173 - 36 holes	Willie Dunn	Newport GC, Newport, R.I.
1896	James Foulis	152 - 36 holes	Horace Rawlins	Shinnecock Hills GC, Southampton, N.Y.
1897	Joe Lloyd	162 - 36 holes	Willie Anderson	Chicago GC, Wheaton, Ill.
1898	Fred Herd	328 - 72 holes	Alex Smith	Myopia Hunt Club, S. Hamilton, Mass.
1899	Willie Smith	315	George Low Val Fitzjohn W.H. Way	Baltimore CC, Baltimore, Md.
1900	Harry Vardon	313	J.H. Taylor	Chicago GC, Wheaton, Ill.
1901	*Willie Anderson (85)	331	Alex Smith (86)	Myopia Hunt Club, S. Hamilton, Mass.
1902	Laurie Auchterlonie	307	Stewart Gardner	Garden City GC, Garden City, N.Y.
1903	*Willie Anderson (82)	307	David Brown (84)	Baltusrol GC, Springfield, N.J.
1904	Willie Anderson	303	Gil Nicholls	Glen View Club, Golf, Ill.
1905	Willie Anderson	314	Alex Smith	Myopia Hunt Club, S. Hamilton, Mass.
1906	Alex Smith	295	Willie Smith	Onwentsia Club, Lake Forest, Ill.
1907	Alex Ross	302	Gil Nicholls	Philadelphia Cricket Club, Chestnut Hill, Pa.
1908	*Fred McLeod (77)	322	Willie Smith (83)	Myopia Hunt Club, S. Hamilton, Mass.
1909	George Sargent	290	Tom McNamara	Englewood GC, Englewood, N.J.
1910	*Alex Smith (71)	298	John J. McDermott (75) Macdonald Smith (77)	Philadelphia Cricket Club, Chestnut Hill, Pa.
1911	*John J. McDermott (80)	307	Michael J. Brady (82) George O. Simpson (85)	Chicago GC, Wheaton, Ill.
1912	John J. McDermott	294	Tom McNamara	CC of Buffalo, Buffalo, N.Y.
1913	*Francis Ouimet (72)	304	Harry Vardon (77) Edward Ray (78)	The Country Club, Brookline, Mass.
1914	Walter Hagen	290	Charles Evans Jr.	Midlothian CC, Blue Island, Ill.
1915	Jerome D. Travers	297	Tom McNamara	Baltusrol GC, Springfield, N.J.
1916	Charles Evans Jr.	286	Jock Hutchinson	Minikahda Club, Minneapolis, Minn.
1917-18	No Championships Played — World War I			
1919	*Walter Hagen (77)	301	Michael J. Brady (78)	Brae Burn CC, West Newton, Mass.
1920	Edward Ray	295	Harry Vardon Jack Burke, Sr. Leo Diegel Jock Hutchison	Inverness Club, Toledo, Ohio
1921	James M. Barnes	289	Walter Hagen Fred McLeod	Columbia CC, Chevy Chase, Md.
1922	Gene Sarazen	288	John L. Black Robert T. Jones Jr.	Skokie CC, Glencoe, Ill.
1923	*Robert T. Jones Jr. (76)	296	Bobby Cruickshank (78)	Inwood CC, Inwood, N.Y.
1924	Cyril Walker	297	Robert T. Jones Jr.	Oakland Hills CC, Birmingham, Mich.
1925	*William Macfarlane (147)	291	Robert T. Jones Jr. (148)	Worcester CC, Worcester, Mass.
1926	Robert T. Jones Jr.	293	Joe Turnesa	Scioto CC, Columbus, Ohio
1927	*Tommy Armour (76)	301	Harry Cooper (79)	Oakmont CC, Oakmont, Pa.
1928	*Johnny Farrell (143)	294	Robert T. Jones Jr. (144)	Olympia Fields CC, Matteson, Ill.

Date	Winner	Score	Runner-Up	Venue
1929	*Robert T. Jones Jr. (141)	294	Al Espinosa (164)	Winged Foot GC, Mamaroneck, N.Y.
1930	Robert T. Jones Jr.	287	Macdonald Smith	Interlachen CC, Hopkins, Minn.
1931	*Billy Burke (149-148)	292	George Von Elm (149-149)	Inverness Club, Toledo, Ohio
1932	Gene Sarazen	286	Phil Perkins	Fresh Meadows CC, Flushing, N.Y.
			Bobby Cruickshank	
1933	Johnny Goodman	287	Ralph Guldahl	North Shore CC, Glenview, Ill.
1934	Olin Dutra	293	Gene Sarazen	Merion Cricket Club, Ardmore, Pa.
1935	Sam Parks Jr.	299	Jimmy Thomson	Oakmont CC, Oakmont, Pa.
1936	Tony Manero	282	Harry Cooper	Baltusrol GC, Springfield, N.J.
1937	Ralph Guldahl	281	Sam Snead	Oakland Hills CC, Birmingham, Mich.
1938	Ralph Guldahl	284	Dick Metz	Cherry Hills CC, Englewood, Col.
1939	*Byron Nelson (68-70)	284	Craig Wood (68-73)	Philadelphia CC, West
			Denny Shute (76)	Conshohocken, Pa.
1940	*Lawson Little (70)	287	Gene Sarazen (73)	Canterbury GC, Cleveland, Ohio
1941	Craig Wood	284	Denny Shute	Colonial Club, Fort Worth, Texas
1942-45	No Championships Played — World War II			
1946	*Lloyd Mangrum (72-72)	284	Vic Ghezzi (72-73)	Canterbury GC, Cleveland, Ohio
			Byron Nelson (72-73)	
1947	*Lew Worsham (69)	282	Sam Snead (70)	St. Louis CC, Clayton, Mo.
1948	Ben Hogan	276	Jimmy Demaret	Riviera CC, Los Angeles, Calif.
1949	Cary Middlecoff	286	Sam Snead	Medinah CC, Medinah, Ill.
			Clayton Heafner	
1950	*Ben Hogan (69)	287	Lloyd Mangrum (73)	Merion GC, Ardmore, Pa.
			George Fazio (75)	
1951	Ben Hogan	287	Clayton Heafner	Oakland Hills CC, Birmingham, Mich.
1952	Julius Boros	281	Ed (Porky) Oliver	Northwood CC, Dallas, Texas
1953	Ben Hogan	283	Sam Snead	Oakmont CC, Oakmont, Pa.
1954	Ed Furgol	284	Gene Littler	Baltusrol GC, Springfield, N.J.
1955	*Jack Fleck (69)	287	Ben Hogan (72)	The Olympic Club, San Francisco, Calif.
1956	Cary Middlecoff	281	Ben Hogan	Oak Hill CC, Rochester, N.Y.
			Julius Boros	
1957	*Dick Mayer (72)	282	Cary Middlecoff (79)	Inverness Club, Toledo, Ohio
1958	Tommy Bolt	283	Gary Player	Southern Hills CC, Tulsa, Okla.
1959	Billy Casper	282	Bob Rosburg	Winged Foot GC, Mamaroneck, N.Y.
1960	Arnold Palmer	280	Jack Nicklaus	Cherry Hills CC, Englewood, Col.
1961	Gene Littler	281	Bob Goalby	Oakland Hills CC, Birmingham, Mich.
			Doug Sanders	
1962	*Jack Nicklaus (71)	283	Arnold Palmer (74)	Oakmont CC, Oakmont, Pa.
1963	*Julius Boros (70)	293	Jacky Cupit (73)	The Country Club, Brookline, Mass.
			Arnold Palmer (76)	
1964	Ken Venturi	278	Tommy Jacobs	Congressional CC, Bethesda, Md.
1965	*Gary Player (71)	282	Kel Nagle (74)	Bellerive CC, St. Louis, Mo.
1966	*Billy Casper (69)	278	Arnold Palmer (73)	The Olympic Club, San Francisco, Calif.
1967	Jack Nicklaus	275	Arnold Palmer	Baltusrol GC, Springfield, N.J.
1968	Lee Trevino	275	Jack Nicklaus	Oak Hill CC, Rochester, N.Y.
1969	Orville Moody	281	Deane Beman	Champions GC, Houston, Texas
			Al Geiberger	
			Bob Rosburg	
1970	Tony Jacklin	281	Dave Hill	Hazeltine National GC, Chaska, Minn.
1971	*Lee Trevino (68)	280	Jack Nicklaus (71)	Merion GC, Ardmore, Pa.
1972	Jack Nicklaus	290	Bruce Crampton	Pebble Beach GL, Pebble Beach, Calif.
1973	Johnny Miller	279	John Schlee	Oakmont CC, Oakmont, Pa.

Date	Winner	Score	Runner-Up	Venue
1974	Hale Irwin	287	Forrest Fezler	Winged Foot GC, Mamaroneck, N.Y.
1975	*Lou Graham (71)	287	John Mahaffey (73)	Medinah CC, Medinah, Ill.
1976	Jerry Pate	277	Tom Weiskopf	Atlanta Athletic Club, Duluth, Ga.
			Al Geiberger	
1977	Hubert Green	278	Lou Graham	Southern Hills CC, Tulsa, Okla.
1978	Andy North	285	Dave Stockton	Cherry Hills CC, Englewood, Col.
			J.C. Snead	
1979	Hale Irwin	284	Gary Player	Inverness Club, Toledo, Ohio
			Jerry Pate	
1980	Jack Nicklaus	272	Isao Aoki	Baltusrol GC, Springfield, N.J.
1981	David Graham	273	George Burns	Merion GC, Ardmore, Pa.
			Bill Rogers	
1982	Tom Watson	282	Jack Nicklaus	Pebble Beach GL, Pebble Beach, Calif.
1983	Larry Nelson	280	Tom Watson	Oakmont CC, Oakmont, Pa.
1984	*Fuzzy Zoeller (67)	276	Greg Norman (75)	Winged Foot GC, Mamaroneck, N.Y.
1985	Andy North	279	Dave Barr	Oakland Hills CC, Birmingham, Mich.
			Chen Tze Chung	
			Denis Watson	
1986	Raymond Floyd	279	Lanny Wadkins	Shinnecock Hills GC,
			Chip Beck	Southampton, N.Y.
1987	Scott Simpson	277	Tom Watson	The Olympic Club, San Francisco, Calif.
1988	*Curtis Strange (71)	278	Nick Faldo (75)	The Country Club, Brookline, Mass.
1989	Curtis Strange	278	Chip Beck	Oak Hill CC, Rochester, N.Y.
			Mark McCumber	
			Ian Woosnam	
1990	*Hale Irwin (74+3)	280	Mike Donald (74+4)	Medinah CC, Medinah, Ill.
1991	*Payne Stewart (75)	282	Scott Simpson (77)	Hazeltine National GC, Chaska, Minn.
1992	Tom Kite	285	Jeff Sluman	Pebble Beach GL, Pebble Beach, Calif.
1993	Lee Janzen	272	Payne Stewart	Baltusrol GC, Springfield, N.J.
1994	*Ernie Els (74+4+4)	279	Loren Roberts (74+4+5)	Oakmont CC, Oakmont, Pa.
			Colin Montgomerie (78)	
1995	Corey Pavin	280	Greg Norman	Shinnecock Hills GC, Southampton, N.Y.
1996	Steve Jones	278	Tom Lehman	Oakland Hills CC, Birmingham, Mich.
			Davis Love III	
1997	Ernie Els	276	Colin Montgomerie	Congressional CC, Bethesda, Md.
1998	Lee Janzen	280	Payne Stewart	The Olympic Club, San Francisco, Calif.
1999	Payne Stewart	279	Phil Mickelson	Pinehurst No. 2, Pinehurst, N.C.
2000	Tiger Woods	272	Miguel Angel Jimenez	Pebble Beach GL, Pebble Beach, Calif.
			Ernie Els	
2001	*Retief Goosen (70)	276	Mark Brooks (72)	Southern Hills CC, Tulsa, Okla.
2002	Tiger Woods	277	Phil Mickelson	Bethpage State Park, Farmingdale, N.Y.

*Winner in playoff; figures in parentheses indicate scores

102nd
U.S. OPEN
Championship Records

Oldest champion *(years/months/days)*
45/0/15 — Hale Irwin (1990)

Youngest champion
19/10/14 — John J. McDermott (1911)

Most victories
4 — Willie Anderson (1901, '03, '04, '05)
4 — Robert T. Jones Jr. (1923, '26, '29, '30)
4 — Ben Hogan (1948, '50, '51, '53)
4 — Jack Nicklaus (1962, '67, '72, '80)
3 — Hale Irwin (1974, '79, '90)
2 — by 15 players: Alex Smith (1906, '10), John J. McDermott (1911, '12), Walter Hagen (1914, '19), Gene Sarazen (1922, '32), Ralph Guldahl (1937, '38), Cary Middlecoff (1949, '56), Julius Boros (1952, '63), Billy Casper (1959, '66), Lee Trevino (1968, '71), Andy North (1978, '85), Curtis Strange (1988, '89), Ernie Els (1994, '97), Lee Janzen (1993, '98), Payne Stewart (1991, '99), and Tiger Woods (2000, '02).

Consecutive victories
Willie Anderson (1903, '04, '05)
John J. McDermott (1911, '12)
Robert T. Jones Jr. (1929, '30)
Ralph Guldahl (1937, '38)
Ben Hogan (1950, '51)
Curtis Strange (1988, '89)

Most times runner-up
4 — Sam Snead
4 — Robert T. Jones Jr.
4 — Arnold Palmer
4 — Jack Nicklaus

Longest course
7,214 yards — Bethpage State Park (Black Course), Farmingdale, N.Y. (2002)

Shortest course
Since World War II
6,528 yards — Merion GC (East Course), Ardmore, Pa. (1971, '81)

Most often host club of Open
7 — Baltusrol GC, Springfield, N.J. (1903, '15, '36, '54, '67, '80, '93)
7 — Oakmont (Pa.) CC (1927, '35, '53, '62, '73, '83, '94)

Largest entry
8,468 (2002)

Smallest entry
11 (1895)

Lowest score, 72 holes
272 — Jack Nicklaus (63-71-70-68), at Baltusrol GC (Lower Course), Springfield, N.J. (1980)
272 — Lee Janzen (67-67-69-69), at Baltusrol GC (Lower Course), Springfield, N.J. (1993)
272 — Tiger Woods (65-69-71-67), at Pebble Beach GL, Pebble Beach, Calif. (2000)

Lowest score, first 54 holes
203 — George Burns (69-66-68), at Merion GC (East Course), Ardmore, Pa. (1981)
203 — Tze-Chung Chen (65-69-69), at Oakland Hills CC (South Course), Birmingham, Mich. (1985)
203 — Lee Janzen (67-67-69), at Baltusrol GC (Lower Course), Springfield, N.J. (1993)

Lowest score, last 54 holes
203 — Loren Roberts (69-64-70), at Oakmont CC, Oakmont, Pa. (1994)

Lowest score, first 36 holes
134 — Jack Nicklaus (63-71), at Baltusrol GC (Lower Course), Springfield, N.J. (1980)
134 — Chen Tze-Chung (65-69), at Oakland Hills CC (South Course), Birmingham, Mich. (1985)
134 — Lee Janzen (67-67), at Baltusrol GC (Lower Course), Springfield, N.J. (1993)
134 — Tiger Woods (65-69), at Pebble Beach GL, Pebble Beach, Calif. (2000)

Lowest score, last 36 holes
132 — Larry Nelson (65-67), at Oakmont CC, Oakmont, Pa. (1983)

Lowest score, 9 holes
29 — Neal Lancaster (second nine, fourth round) at Shinnecock Hills GC, Southampton, N.Y. (1995)
29 — Neal Lancaster (second nine, second round) at Oakland Hills CC, Birmingham, Mich. (1996)

Lowest score, 18 holes
63 — Johnny Miller, fourth round at Oakmont CC, Oakmont, Pa. (1973)
63 — Jack Nicklaus, first round at Baltusrol GC (Lower Course), Springfield, N.J. (1980)
63 — Tom Weiskopf, first round at Baltusrol GC (Lower Course), Springfield, N.J. (1980)

Largest winning margin
15 — Tiger Woods (272), at Pebble Beach GL, Pebble Beach Calif. (2000)

Highest winning score
Since World War II
293 — Julius Boros, at The Country Club, Brookline, Mass. (1963) (won in playoff)

Best start by champion
63 — Jack Nicklaus, at Baltusrol GC (Lower Course), Springfield, N.J. (1980)

Best finish by champion
63 — Johnny Miller, at Oakmont (Pa.) CC (1973)

Worst start by champion
Since World War II
76 — Ben Hogan, at Oakland Hills CC (South Course), Birmingham, Mich. (1951)

76 — Jack Fleck, at The Olympic Club (Lake Course), San Francisco, Calif. (1955)

Worst finish by champion
Since World War II

75 — Cary Middlecoff, at Medinah CC (No. 3 Course), Medinah, Ill. (1949)

75 — Hale Irwin, at Inverness Club, Toledo, Ohio (1979)

Lowest score to lead field, 18 holes

63 — Jack Nicklaus and Tom Weiskopf, at Baltusrol GC (Lower Course), Springfield, N.J. (1980)

Lowest score to lead field, 36 holes

134 — Jack Nicklaus (63-71), at Baltusrol GC (Lower Course), Springfield, N.J. (1980)

134 — Chen Tze-Chung (65-69), at Oakland Hills CC (South Course), Birmingham, Mich. (1985)

134 — Lee Janzen (67-67), at Baltusrol GC (Lower Course), Springfield, N.J. (1993)

134 — Tiger Woods (65-69), at Pebble Beach GL, Pebble Beach, Calif. (2000)

Lowest score to lead field, 54 holes

203 — George Burns (69-66-68), at Merion GC (East Course), Ardmore, Pa. (1981)

203 — Chen Tze-Chung (65-69-69), at Oakland Hills CC (South Course), Birmingham, Mich. (1985)

203 — Lee Janzen (67-67-69), at Baltusrol GC (Lower Course), Springfield, N.J. (1993)

Highest score to lead field, 18 holes
Since World War II

71 — Sam Snead, at Oakland Hills CC (South Course), Birmingham, Mich. (1951)

71 — Tommy Bolt, Julius Boros, and Dick Metz, at Southern Hills CC, Tulsa, Okla. (1958)

71 — Tony Jacklin, at Hazeltine National GC, Chaska, Minn. (1970)

71 — Orville Moody, Jack Nicklaus, Chi Chi Rodriguez, Mason Rudolph, Tom Shaw, and Kermit Zarley, at Pebble Beach (Calif.) Golf Links (1972)

Highest score to lead field, 36 holes
Since World War II

144 — Bobby Locke (73-71), at Oakland Hills CC (South Course), Birmingham, Mich. (1951)

144 — Tommy Bolt (67-77) and E. Harvie Ward (74-70), at The Olympic Club (Lake Course), San Francisco, Calif. (1955)

144 — Homero Blancas (74-70), Bruce Crampton (74-70), Jack Nicklaus (71-73), Cesar Seduno (72-72), Lanny Wadkins (76-68) and Kermit Zarley (71-73), at Pebble Beach (Calif.) Golf Links (1972)

Highest score to lead field, 54 holes
Since World War II

218 — Bobby Locke (73-71-74), at Oakland Hills CC (South Course), Birmingham, Mich. (1951)

218 — Jacky Cupit (70-72-76), at The Country Club, Brookline, Mass. (1963)

Highest 36-hole cut

155 — at The Olympic Club (Lakeside Course), San Francisco, Calif. (1955)

Most players to tie for lead, 18 holes

7 — at Pebble Beach (Calif.) Golf Links (1972); at Southern Hills CC, Tulsa, Okla. (1977); and at Shinnecock Hills GC, Southampton, N.Y. (1896)

Most players to tie for lead, 36 holes

6 — at Pebble Beach (Calif.) Golf Links (1972)

Most players to tie for lead, 54 holes

4 — at Oakmont (Pa.) CC (1973)

Most sub-par rounds, championship

124 — at Medinah CC (No. 3 Course), Medinah, Ill. (1990)

Most sub-par 72-hole totals, championship

28 — at Medinah CC (No. 3 Course), Medinah, Ill. (1990)

Most sub-par scores, first round

39 — at Medinah CC (No. 3 Course), Medinah, Ill. (1990)

Most sub-par scores, second round

47 — at Medinah CC (No. 3 Course), Medinah, Ill. (1990)

Most sub-par scores, third round

24 — at Medinah CC (No. 3 Course), Medinah, Ill. (1990)

Most sub-par scores, fourth round

18 — at Baltusrol GC (Lower Course), Springfield, N.J. (1993)

Most sub-par rounds by one player in one championship

4 — Billy Casper, at The Olympic Club (Lakeside Course), San Francisco, Calif. (1966)

4 — Lee Trevino, at Oak Hill CC (East Course), Rochester, N.Y. (1968)

4 — Tony Jacklin, at Hazeltine National GC, Chaska, Minn. (1970)

4 — Lee Janzen, at Baltusrol GC (Lower Course), Springfield, N.J. (1993)

Highest score, one hole

19 — Ray Ainsley, at the 16th (par 4) at Cherry Hills CC, Englewood, Col. (1938)

Most consecutive birdies

6 — George Burns (holes 2–7), at Pebble Beach (Calif.) Golf Links (1972) and Andy Dillard (holes 1-6), at Pebble Beach (Calif.) Golf Links (1992)

Most consecutive 3s

7 — Hubert Green (holes 10–16), at Southern Hills Country Club, Tulsa, Okla. (1977)

7 — Peter Jacobsen (holes 1–7), at The Country Club, Brookline, Mass. (1988)

Most consecutive Opens

44 — Jack Nicklaus (1957-2000)

Most Opens completed 72 holes

35 — Jack Nicklaus

Most consecutive Opens completed 72 holes

22 — Walter Hagen (1913-36; no Championships 1917-18)

22 — Gene Sarazen (1920-41)

22 — Gary Player (1958-79)

Robert Sommers is the former editor and publisher of the USGA's *Golf Journal*, author of *The U.S. Open: Golf's Ultimate Challenge* and *Golf Anecdotes*. He is based in Port St. Lucie, Fla.

Michael Cohen is a photographer based in New York City and a contributor to many magazines and books.

Phil Inglis is a photographer based in England and a contributor to many publications.

Par and Yardage

Hole	Par	Yardage	Hole	Par	Yardage
1	4	430	10	4	492
2	4	389	11	4	435
3	3	205	12	4	499
4	5	517	13	5	554
5	4	451	14	3	161
6	4	408	15	4	459
7	4	489	16	4	479
8	3	210	17	3	207
9	4	418	18	4	411
	35	3,517		35	3,697
				70	7,214